W9-CSN-250

Character Is Destiny

The Value of Personal Ethics in Everyday Life

RUSSELL W. GOUGH

CROWN FORUM
NEW YORK

Published by Crown Forum, New York, New York. Member of the Crown Publishing Group, a division of Random House, Inc.
www.crownpublishing.com

Originally published by Prima Publishing, Roseville, California, in 1997.

Printed in the United States of America

Library of Congress Cataloging-in-Publication Data
Gough, Russell Wayne.
Character is destiny : the value of personal ethics in everyday life. / Russell Gough.
p. cm.
Includes bibliographical references.
1. Character. I. Title.
BJ1521.G64 1997
170'.44—dc21 97-18973
CIP

ISBN 0-7615-1163-6

10 9 8 7
First Edition

To Jeannine, Nicholas, and Gabriella: my beloved wife and children, my gifts from God, my precious family; the *sine qua non* of my life, my happiness, my destiny

Contents

Foreword

T.S. Eliot once observed that some of his contemporaries were in the habit of "dreaming of systems so perfect that no one will need to be good." The dream of finding a substitute for character is still, of course, very much alive. After all, being good is hard work. How much better if, by some happy arrangement, society could discover the right technical or governmental solution to problems such as incivility, crime, drug abuse, and irresponsible sex. A number of these technical solutions have already been tried—clean needles, Norplant, safe-sex kits, gun exchange programs, and the like—but they never seem to improve our situation. And they never manage to relieve us of our responsibilities.

The dream of a society "so perfect that no one will need to be good" is really a child's dream. It betrays a hope that the "grownups" (society, the government) will take care of everything so the rest of us can just play. This is exactly the kind of attitude we might expect to arise in a culture where so many people are in search of their own inner child. And it helps to explain why, when hurt in the pursuit of play and pleasure, so many look for someone else—a corporation, a product manufacturer—to blame.

We need to stop dreaming. The truth is, there is no substitute for personal character and there never will be. By the same token, there is no way to educate young people for character in the absence of adults with character. Character development is not something the schools can do through the introduction of some new, technically perfect curriculum. Rather, the best way for a young person to learn good habits of behavior is by identifying with and imitating adults who already practice those habits. By making *adult* character education its primary focus, *Character Is Destiny* reminds us that the process of cultivating virtue and overcoming vice in one's personal character does not—should not—end simply because one has entered adulthood. Indeed, it reminds us that being of adult age is one thing, but actually *being adult,* in the sense of exemplifying moral maturity as a matter of regular practice, is quite another. And perhaps more tellingly, it reminds us that no matter who we are and no matter how ethically comfortable or self-satisfied we have become, all of us fall far short of perfection, and thus should steadfastly keep striving to become fully grown moral beings.

What does it mean, from a moral point of view, to be an adult? *Charakter,* the word Aristotle uses to describe moral maturity, means "enduring marks." There is something lasting about a person of character. He or she does not change with the seasons, is not, in Shakespeare's words, "a pipe for fortune's finger to sound what stop she please." To help us understand the term better, Professor Gough makes a useful distinction between *character* and *personality* (a word with which our society is far more comfortable). What's the difference between the two? Consider the following poem:

> Out upon it! I have loved
> Three whole days together;
> And am like to love three more,
> If it prove fair weather.

We can easily detect a personality here. The narrator of Sir John Suckling's seventeenth-century poem seems to have plenty of that. He strikes us as bold, engaging, humorous—the sort we refer to as a lovable rogue. But it's hard to detect any enduring traits of character in this "constant lover." A charming personality, perhaps, but, in other respects, reliably unreliable.

There are countless books available to tell us how to develop a more charming or persuasive personality, but few that tell us how we can acquire the more important traits of good character—the kind of traits that make it possible to be a "constant lover" in the true sense, or to be a constant and committed parent. But *Character Is Destiny* is more than a how-to book. Professor Gough provides us not only with commonsense practices, but also the commonsense philosophy that infuses practice with meaning. Moreover, he is aware of the self-defeating attitudes we often employ: "That's just the way I am," "I'm too set in my ways to change," or "You can't teach an old dog new tricks." Refreshingly, *Character Is Destiny* rejects such moral evasions, and replaces them with pragmatic guidelines for pursuing and cultivating virtue.

Equally refreshing, *Character Is Destiny* sticks to its subject. Now that politicians have discovered "character" and "virtue," the terms have become a bit suspect. The inevitable question that occurs is, "Is there some hidden agenda here?" Is this a book about political ideology? About being conservative or liberal? The answer to these questions is no. Rather, it's simply, though profoundly, about being a person of *good character,* a person of *virtue.* And people of good character and virtue, of course, can and do give allegiance to any number of political parties and persuasions. We all know people who, though we may agree with them on the issues of the day, are people we can never really trust. Conversely, we all know others who we trust implicitly even though we don't see eye-to-eye on politics. This book's sole allegiance is to the ethical character that allows all people, regardless of political persuasion, to live lives of integrity. And in so doing it is a book for *everybody,* precisely because it speaks to us on the most fundamental level—as free moral agents.

We owe Russell Gough a debt of gratitude for making clear what most "experts" in character education fail to realize: We become better people not by discussing ethics, but by practicing good behavior. In this profound yet practical book, Gough reminds us that the hard part of morality is not knowing what is right, but doing what is right. Is doing the right thing something we can learn in three easy steps? No, says Professor Gough, but the good news is that, with time and practice, acting with courage, fairness, and self-control becomes increasingly natural and effortless. This is an important contribution to the national debate about character. And, equally important, it's the kind of book that can make a real difference in the life of the reader.

WILLIAM KILPATRICK

Preface

While writing this book, I experienced two unforgettable incidents—one inspiring, the other disheartening. Both are related to the themes presented in *Character Is Destiny,* and both will remain indelibly etched in my memory. I'll briefly describe these two incidents, beginning with the disheartening, more recent one.

As I was putting the finishing touches on the final manuscript, just before it went to press, something happened that spoke volumes to me. It should speak volumes to all of us about our culture's desperate need for honest, soul-searching discussions of personal ethics and character. For the first time in my teaching career, a student threatened to take legal action against me over a failing grade deservedly received in one of my courses.

What a lamentable sign of the times: a student threatening to take a teacher to court over a grade! And what bitter, sobering irony it involved, for this student had at one time written eloquently and insightfully about the very themes discussed in this book. For me, I must confess, it was a shrill wake-up call concerning two serious issues: how far many of us are willing to go to avoid taking responsibility for our own actions, and how deeply our culture's win-at-all-costs attitude has eroded our belief in the primary importance of integrity and personal character.

While there were no valid grounds for legal action against me, I can't deny that I found the mere threat of a lawsuit quite unsettling. (In fact, this represented the first and only time anyone has ever threatened me with a lawsuit for any reason.) What I found most disconcerting was that the student and family behind the threat were by all accounts—including my own—good and decent people. Indeed, they *are* good and decent people, practicing Christians, people whom most of us would be happy to have as friends or neighbors.

Why would good and decent people—like you and me—do such a thing? That's one of the critical questions I've tried to address in this book.

The second remarkable thing that happened while writing this book occurred just as I was completing the rough, original manuscript. It was during one of those times when a writer has second thoughts about the ultimate value of his or her project, especially one such as this book. Is this book worth reading? Will people really be interested in a book about personal ethics and character? If they do read it, will they be better in the least for having done so?

I was asking myself questions such as these in late August 1996. It was the beginning of a new school year, and I was about to deliver a keynote lecture on personal ethics and character to Pepperdine's incoming freshman students (as I have been doing for several years). Immediately following my lecture to the new freshman class, two colleagues of mine, Bob White and Hung Le (the two administrators who have honored me by continually inviting me to deliver this keynote lecture), related a story that dramatically reassured me of the potential value of this book.

After Bob and Hung offered their usual, gracious words of thanks and compliments, they proceeded to tell me of a graduate who had recently faced an unenviable and gut-wrenching ethical dilemma at work. This woman had learned of a blatantly illegal and unethical company practice, and had been told by her high-level manager that if she blew the whistle she would not only be fired but would also be blackballed forever in that particular industry.

This was a serious threat and one the woman was sure the manager would carry out. Her family as well as her closest friends strongly encouraged her to think long and hard about the consequences of blowing the whistle. After all, her present (and future) career was at stake.

Valiantly, and with a noble, come-what-may attitude, she decided to ignore the manager's warning and expose the wrongful business practice. To her great and unexpected relief (albeit after several days of agonizing uncertainty over the fate of her career), the company's high executives ended up supporting her. She kept her job, and the high-level manager was demoted.

Throughout the whole ordeal, the woman had been in touch regularly with Bob and Hung, both of whom had given her support as friends and sources of moral strength. The main reason Bob and Hung were so intent on sharing this woman's story with me is because in coming to her decision and in its defense, she had expressly invoked my name and "with passionate conviction in her voice" had cited from memory a few of the principles expressed in this book.

This revelation moved me deeply. It's not very often that a teacher—much less a professor of ethics—hears such reassuring testimonials from his or her students. The secondhand testimonial not only gave this author a shot in the arm but also touched this teacher's heart.

Thus, of the several people to whom I owe a special word of appreciation, I would like to begin by thanking Bob and Hung—and that anonymous former student—for their timely encouragement, given to me when I probably needed it the most. But, come to think of it, that's just like Bob and Hung—*always* offering much-needed words of encouragement and support to others.

With respect to the individuals who have been directly involved with the production and promotion of this book, I have been particularly fortunate. And my good fortune is not simply due to the fact that they are all quintessential professionals, which they certainly are. It is also and more importantly due to the fact that they have invariably expressed their sincere belief in, and the need for, this book's message. So to my agent, Carol Mann, and her associate, Christy Fletcher, and to the team at Prima Publishing—Ben Dominitz, Steven Martin, Betsy Towner, Kathryn Hashimoto, and Patty Oien—I would like to offer my sincere thanks for their exemplary competence and support.

Second only to my wife (and that's saying a great deal!), there are four people to whom I am especially—and continually—indebted: David Baird, John Secia, Jeff Bliss, and Don Jacobs. Regarding virtually all of my teaching, speaking, and writing about ethics and character, they are friends, colleagues, and even fans in the highest sense of these terms. For their heartfelt and "headfelt" support, I am truly thankful.

Last, and as always, I wish to express my undying gratitude to Jeannine, my wife, most-valued friend, and role model *par excellence.* For her unfailing love and encouragement, and particularly for the sacrifices she so willingly makes to enable me to complete a project such as this one, I am deeply appreciative and forever in her debt. I love her with all my heart, and, given Jeannine's diamondlike character as well as my indebtedness to her, it is only fitting that *Character Is Destiny* be dedicated to her honor.

Introduction

No one would want
to live without friends.

Aristotle

A personal conversation between friends about personal character: That, in a nutshell, describes the spirit in which I have written this book.

By using the expression "between friends," I'm not trying to be either cute or quaint. Quite the contrary, my intent is both sincere and high-minded, and it is not unlike the spirit in which the ancient Greek philosopher Aristotle wrote about friendship over 2,300 years ago.

In his *Nichomachean Ethics*, still widely regarded as the most complete book ever written on the subject of ethics and character, Aristotle devoted the single greatest portion of the work—nearly one-fourth—to a discussion of friendship.

"But why," you might be wondering, "would he spend so much time talking about friendship in a book about ethics and character?"

Aristotle's answer to this question is anything but obsolete or archaic, and it in fact offers those of us at the dawning of the twenty-first century a refreshing and much-needed perspective on the profound *ethical* dimension of true friendship. For Aristotle, the truest friendship is far more than mere companionship, mutual hobbies, and a common network of acquaintances. Friends in the highest sense of the term are those who make a conscientious effort to take ethics and personal character seriously and inspire each other to be better—in thought, in action, in life.

Indeed, for Aristotle, as for all the great moral thinkers throughout human history, nothing could be more important in the quest to improve our individual lives or our society than giving serious attention to personal character.

I'm going to make the point even more boldly. It is *impossible* to improve our individual lives or our society without genuinely caring about and striving to improve personal character. You must genuinely care about your personal character, I must genuinely care about mine, and we must genuinely care about each other's—as "friends."

I do hope you find the last two sentiments provocative, but please don't assume that I've made them merely to pique your interest or that I'm exaggerating for melodramatic effect. Let me be clear from the start: If I did not believe in the literal truth of these sentiments, I would not have written this book.

There is now hardly a day that goes by in which I am not reminded of these ideas' consequential truth. Sometimes the reminders come in big and dramatic ways;

more often they come in small ways. And sometimes—too often, I must admit—they come in painfully acute fashion, meaning that a weakness of my own personal character has somehow generated the reminder.

This frequently happens when I'm driving on southern California's congested freeways, a less-than-enjoyable daily experience that has come to be one of my most challenging character tests. I won't beat around the bush: I hate traffic and I hate to be late; more to the point, I'm far from being a patient driver in heavy traffic, and my impatience has led to embarrassing and inexcusable acts of disrespect and incivility on more than one occasion. When another driver cuts me off, tailgates, or crawls along under the speed limit in the fast lane, it is *not* my habit to take it in stride, keep it in perspective, and remain calm, to say the least. My first and strong inclination is not merely to lay on my horn but to roll down my window, shout demeaning insults, and generally emote in ways that I would be absolutely mortified for family, friends, and colleagues to hear about, much less witness.

This may bring a smile to your face or may even make you laugh out loud, either because, like me, you've "been there, done that" (or *are* there and *are* doing that!), or simply because you can visualize witnessing someone like me behaving like a raving lunatic at 6:45 A.M., in bumper-to-bumper traffic, for no good reason. However, from the standpoint of ethics and character, everyday events like this are neither trivial nor humorous.

As we will see in our conversation to follow, such commonplace, day-to-day scenarios—whether at home, work, play, or in transit—represent windows into our personal characters: windows that can show us, if we look honestly and carefully, the general shape and direction of our individual "destinies"; windows that can reveal to us our deep-seated weaknesses (and strengths) of character. What I would especially like to drive home is how our weaknesses of character—often leading us to do and say things that are regrettable, hurtful, and downright wrong—can be overcome and displaced with strong virtues of character, *if* we genuinely desire to improve ourselves and are willing to work hard at it.

I often tell the story of a twenty-something baseball player who sincerely tried to convince me that he had no control over his explosive temper, specifically when an umpire had made a bad or merely questionable call. The player wasn't trying to argue that he shouldn't be punished for bumping or screaming demeaning expletives at umpires; he was simply arguing that he was short-tempered "by nature" and that his bad temper was thus uncontrollable. So I bluntly asked him, "In these situations, why don't you just take your bat and beat the umpire over the head to a bloody pulp so that he won't ever be able to make another bad or questionable call?" The baseball player, of course, was quite shocked by my question, and replied, "How can you even suggest such a thing? I couldn't possibly do *that!*" To which I then responded, "Well, how is it that you can control your temper at one point but not at another? Doesn't this show that you are squarely in the position of *choosing* at which point you will or will not control your temper? Moreover, would you likewise lose your temper if the umpire happened to be, say, your mother, your boss, or a leader from your church?"

The same point is equally true for me when I'm behind the wheel of my car. One time, just as I was about to boil over and spew at some blankety-blank driver for tailing me, I happened to take a good look in my rearview mirror and noticed that the offending driver was a colleague and good friend of mine. Unsurprisingly, I *immediately* cooled down, composed myself, and a big grin broke forth from my hardened face.

Let's be honest from the onset: Despite the fatalistic, "I can't help it" attitudes so prevalent in our day, the truth is that *we do have control over and can overcome our weaknesses of character.*

Although I have written *Character Is Destiny* at a time when our country is experiencing a welcome and laudable revival of concern for issues of personal ethics and character as well as character education in the schools, I have approached this vital subject matter with the hope that its message will resonate with readers long after politicians and the media have ceased making "character" the latest headline in the national news. We simply cannot afford to allow issues of personal character and ethics to be treated as the latest political trend or fad, as if the timeless importance of these issues simply went in and out of fashion like bell-bottoms and miniskirts.

Nobody knew this better than our country's founding fathers, who were keenly aware of the *essential* value of personal ethics and character, a point they gave great emphasis to in *The Federalist Papers*, a brilliant set of essays written in 1787–88 in defense of the Constitution. Their passionate plea was, and still is, that if the wondrous political experiment called democracy is to succeed, it will require more than any other form of government a higher degree of "virtue"—of ethical character—in its citizens. For you and me and our fellow Americans, the hard-hitting reality of this plea couldn't be more timely or critical.

Of course, when it comes to cultivating virtue, to actually *improving* personal character, the responsibility ultimately lies with each adult individual. You are ultimately responsible for your personal character, as I am for mine.

In this spirit, this book offers what I call a mirroring, rather than a finger-pointing, approach. In one-on-one, conversational fashion, its primary goal is to encourage each of us to think about improving our personal lives and our society exclusively in terms of our own personal character. Not his character. Not her character. Not their characters. Only "my" character.

My aim is not to judge, but to improve; this is an important distinction. If any process of judging is involved, it will only be that which you must honestly and painstakingly do of your own character and actions.

In a similar vein, my aim is not to dwell on our past mistakes. While there is profound truth in the saying "You are your past"—a truth we would be foolish to ignore completely—my emphasis will be more forward looking:

how yesterday has shaped what you are today with a view toward what you can be tomorrow.

To benefit from the conversation in this book, only two things are required on the front end: You must in fact care about the improvement of your personal character and our society in general, and you must be willing to take a serious look in the mirror.

Each chapter in this book is designed to emphasize a given aspect of the all-important nature of personal character. At the same time, each chapter is designed to encourage practical self-reflection and enduring personal growth.

You will notice that each chapter begins with a thought-provoking quote about character. I'm not using these quotes in the usual way, to spice up the beginning of a given discussion. Instead, I'm offering them as actual titles that capture the force and point of each chapter. In this way, you'll find that these chapter titles are definitely well worth committing to memory and, of course, living by.

We live in an exhilarating age of mind-boggling computer technology, an amazing and profitable age that tempts each of us, increasingly and regrettably, to adopt a detached spectator mentality—rather than a full-fledged *participant* mentality. One of my loftier hopes for the book is that it can help counteract the harmful way in which many of us have become accustomed to blaming others for our personal struggles and society's problems. Hopefully we can all begin to take the time to look in the proverbial mirror to ask ourselves questions such as these:

What about *my* character and the attitudes and actions that flow from it?

Could it be that *my* character is partly, if not greatly, responsible for *my* personal struggles and even for *my* society's problems?

Could it be that *my* character is necessarily an important part of the solution to these problems?

Questions such as these are not the least bit trivial. They are monumental—destiny-determining—especially when we bear in mind, as we will in the pages to follow, that it is impossible to improve the circumstances of society or of *my* individual life without genuinely caring about and striving to improve *my* personal character.

CHAPTER ONE

Character is destiny.

Heraclitus

Not your personality, but your character, is destiny.

The distinction is crucial—and making it clear at the very beginning of our discussion is equally crucial, given the ways in which pop psychology has blurred this important distinction over the past fifty years or so.

Chances are that the distinction between personality and character will not be obvious to most people. Today, we often use the two terms interchangeably, such as when we say, "She has this type of character" and "That's just her personality," or when we speak alternatively of "his character traits" and "his personality traits."

Character is by no means used only in the sense we are going to use it—in the ethical sense of what you are in your essence, the sum total of your habits, your personal assortment of virtues and vices. But you may find it interesting to learn that, historically, virtually all cultures across time have used the concept in this way, not just Heraclitus, Aristotle, and their ancient Greek culture in general.

That is, until quite recently, in the middle part of the twentieth century.

Before taking a closer look at some of the present-day confusions that have arisen between character and personality, let's look again at the words of Heraclitus that begin this chapter. To better appreciate the time-honored ethical sense of character, you might find it helpful to see and learn something about Heraclitus' phrase in his own ancient Greek words:

εθος ανθροπος δαιμον
ethos anthropos daimon
(character) (man) (destiny)

Let's look at the three words in reverse order: *daimon* is most often translated as "destiny" or "fate"; *anthropos*, from which we have derived words like "anthropology" and "anthropomorphic," simply means "man." (Thus the phrase is often translated literally as "Man's character is his destiny.")

I especially would like us to focus on that initial word, *ethos*. It's the Greek word from which we have derived our words "ethics" and "ethical" (as well as the English word "ethos"). Four useful points can be made about this word.

First, keep in mind that *ethos* is most often translated as "character."

Second, after taking note of the obvious similarity between *ethos* and our word "ethics," we can begin to appreciate the important extent to which ethics is inextricably intertwined with character, a fact that holds true for both the individual and society: *One's ethics goes hand in hand with one's character.* This truly is an essential point, because many people have gotten the idea that being ethical is just a matter of following rules or laws, like when someone says defensively, "I didn't break any rules, so how in the world can you say I was unethical?" The answer to this question, as we'll see in greater detail in Chapter 12, is "All too easily." In the deepest and most comprehensive ways, ethics is a matter of your personal character, of what kind of person you are inside, and it is not merely a matter of whether you follow the rules (we do, of course, have an important ethical responsibility to follow the rules).

Third, while *ethos* is most often translated as "character," in its most basic sense for Heraclitus and his fellow Greeks, the word meant "habit" or "customary behavior." Thus, without any loss of meaning, we could justifiably translate Heraclitus' phrase as follows: "Habit is destiny" or "Customary behavior is destiny." Or, to use Aristotle's wonderfully concise description of personal character—"We are what we repeatedly do"—we could translate Heraclitus' phrase like this: "What we repeatedly do is destiny."

Fourth, when the ancient Greeks talked about good and bad habits of ethical character, they invariably used words that in English we render as "virtues" and "vices." It is this conception of character—with its deeply ethical connections to one's individual habits, to one's virtues and vices, as well as to one's future—that ancient Greek cultures and virtually all cultures in human history have largely employed.

That is, once again, until quite recently.

It was not until well into the twentieth century, with the development of academic psychology and particularly with the emergence of books about pop psychology and self-improvement, that any confusion arose in everyday usage between the age-old concept of character and what we now call personality.

Mainstream academic psychology has typically kept the notions of character and personality quite distinct in its own research and writings. Since at least the 1930s, in its efforts to become an objective science, academic psychology has almost exclusively talked in terms of personality, realizing that the time-honored notion of character was a richly ethical concept that couldn't be scientifically measured. Psychologists began defining "the self" more narrowly in terms of personality "traits," such as assertiveness, self-esteem, and compulsiveness, and thereby eliminated from their research the more holistic conception of human beings defined in terms of habits of character, such as honesty, respect, and loyalty.

Please don't think that I'm presuming to point a fault-finding finger at academic psychology, as if the discipline did a bad thing when it replaced the notion of character with personality for its research purposes. Toward its goal of being scientific, academic psychology certainly has the right to define narrowly whatever it's trying to investigate. Moreover, I should point out that not everyone in academic psychology uses such narrow conceptions of "self." For example, because of their interest in ethics and moral education, a number of contemporary developmental psychologists continue to utilize the age-old concept of character in their own insightful research and writings.

Nonetheless, problems in our collective understanding and confusions in our language do exist, and they have arisen primarily because of the ways in which academic psychology's notion of personality has been used in the pop psychology, self-help, and "how to be a success in life" literature of the past fifty years or so. I especially have in mind the way this mass-market literature and its narrow psychological concept of personality essentially co-opted the idea of character, stripping the idea of its richly ethical and historical meaning to the point where "character" is now often used as a watered-down synonym for "personality."

So, for example, when we say something like "She has this type of character," we usually will be describing a personality that is, say, energetic and bubbly or quiet and shy. Likewise, when we make a passing remark such as "He's a character," we usually will be pointing to a person's humorous or eccentric personality, a personality that especially sets the person off from other people in a highly distinctive way. And when we speak of character traits, we often use the term in a sense identical to personality traits. (Expressions, by the way, such as "Her strength of character," "He is a person of character," and "She has character" still typically convey some aspect of the age-old meaning of character.)

None of this is meant to suggest that it's somehow wrong to use, as we now often do, traits and habits or personality and character synonymously. We can certainly use these terms as we see fit; after all, they're only words. But this does not change the historical fact that the way we now use these terms interchangeably—and confusingly—is symptomatic of deeper confusions. That's why we need to clarify the distinction early on and why, for the sake of clarity, we will continue to keep these sets of terms separate throughout our discussion.

The upshot of this short exercise in semantics is that many people have unfortunately gotten the impression that *personality is destiny.* That personality is where it's at. That personality is success.

It's not. The age-old notion of character is.

We can't, of course, argue that one's personality has nothing to do with one's destiny or success in life. Your personality traits certainly are a part of who and what you are and what you will become. And, to the extent that your personality—whether extroverted or introverted, confident or not confident, assertive or unassertive, for example—will contribute to the shape, quality, and ultimate direction of your life, I, for one, do not doubt the possibility that you can benefit (or have benefited) personally from any number of popular self-help books.

But it's important to keep in mind that prior to the middle part of this century, what we now think of as personality traits were always embodied in, and were always secondary to, the kind of character you possessed. Embedded in the classic concept of character is the idea that you are much more than your personality traits and much more than the genetic makeup bestowed on you by Mother Nature.

Personality will always be secondary to character when it comes to the shape, quality, and ultimate direction of your life and especially when it comes to the all-important question of how good a person you really are.

That character is more important than personality can easily be seen in the fact that we don't typically hold people responsible for their personality traits, but we certainly do so for their habits of character. We don't, for example, praise or blame someone ethically for being either introverted or extroverted. That, as we say, is just the way a person is, "by nature." But we do praise or blame someone ethically for being honest or dishonest, unselfish or selfish, respectful or disrespectful, trustworthy or untrustworthy.

For all the understandable emphasis and attention that our culture continues to give self-esteem (many people even have the impression that self-esteem is a kind of cure-all personality trait), there is no necessary causal connection between self-esteem and being a good person. In other words, just because a person has a great deal of self-esteem is no guarantee at all that he or she is a good person.

Two brief examples, both worth pondering in and of themselves, can help illustrate this point. In a widely acclaimed investigation of the rescuers of Jews during the Holocaust, it was revealed that many of these heroic rescuers actually had low self-esteem; the researchers ultimately concluded that there was no connection between self-esteem and being a rescuer. Next, consider that a number of contemporary studies have revealed a strong link between high self-esteem and unethical and antisocial behaviors, with the researchers of one recent comprehensive study concluding: "Certain forms of high self-esteem seem to increase one's proneness to violence. An uncritical endorsement of the cultural value of self-esteem may therefore be counterproductive and even dangerous."

My point here is in no way meant to undermine the potential value of self-esteem (or any positive personality traits, for that matter) to make our lives more enjoyable and fulfilling. To the extent that you work on enhancing personality traits like self-esteem in conjunction with efforts to work on habits of character like honesty and self-discipline, you can have a very powerful combination for developing excellent personal character.

My point is essentially this: Human societies, like individual human lives, ultimately depend and flourish not on a foundation of personality traits but on a foundation of habits of character. That's why I stress in the Introduction that it is impossible to improve our individual lives or our society without making personal character a top priority.

Character understood in this way implies the following:

- You, like all human beings, have the capacity to determine who you are or what you want to be—or should be—over and above what you are "by nature."
- What you are in your essence has an inescapable ethical dimension.
- You have the innate ability to *choose* to be good.
- In sum, when it comes to the kind of person you are, you and you alone ultimately determine your own destiny.

With these four central points—the last one in particular—I'm not trying to paint a stark, "bootstrapping" picture of personal growth, as if our character development and our destiny did not at all depend on outside help or influence. In the deepest ways, even as adults, we do need the steadfast encouragement and example of others. And, of course, for many of us, "others" will most importantly entail a divine and transcendent Other—God, the perfect Moral Being who represents the eternal well-spring of goodness, who makes our choice of destinies possible, and without whom there is no hope for a destiny with a capital "D."

The picture of personal character I am attempting to paint gives special and bold emphasis to the reality that, at the most basic level, *you and I as adults cannot blame others for who and what we are.* On the contrary, from the standpoint of personal character, we must take responsibility for who and what we presently are as well as who and what we hope to become. And while our personal growth does indeed require help from others, the fact remains that others, including God, can help us if and only if we are willing to be helped. Therefore, to allow others to help us we must first be willing to help ourselves. Striving to grow—or not—as a person of character is ultimately a choice that is determined by *me.*

CHAPTER TWO

The unexamined life is not worth living.

Socrates

For the title of this chapter, I quote an immortal sentiment expressed by one of the most well known and revered of all philosophers.

Socrates made provocative remarks like this famous one as part of his daily practice in Athens in the late fourth century B.C. (several years after Heraclitus' death). When he made these statements, he was invariably exhorting his fellow Greeks to avoid falling into the trap of what we might call "ethical complacency," the point at which an individual ceases trying to become a better person.

People can become ethically complacent for varying reasons. They might, for example, have become so consumed in their daily lives with making money or gaining fame or enhancing their physical appearance that they are essentially left with no time and energy to think about improving themselves in any other respect. (Ironically, these particular reasons, all too familiar in the present day, were what concerned Socrates most about his fellow Greeks.) Or, people might have developed an "Oh well, I'm too set in my ways now" attitude. Or their attitude might have become one of "I'm content with the way I am, faults and all—so why bother trying to improve anymore?" Or, worst-case scenario, they may simply have come to believe that their character has no room for improvement.

For Socrates, wise, conscientious, and forthright teacher that he was, these "reasons" are really nothing of the sort and are rather best described as excuses or self-deceiving falsehoods, or both. For him, the first and most important part of examining one's life from an ethical perspective—or of appreciating the importance of personal ethics in one's everyday life—is being honest about and taking responsibility for where and what one is as a free, moral, and adult human being.

With his marked emphasis on honest, ethical self-examination, Socrates was also echoing a sacred two-word principle known to virtually every person in the ancient Greek world: "Know yourself." He was not, however, merely echoing this sacred principle; he was deeply transforming its meaning. And herein lies not only the brilliance of Socrates' teaching and example but also an essential starting point for our looking-in-the-mirror discussion.

"Know yourself" was one of two sacred mottoes inscribed over the entrance to the temple of Apollo at Delphi—regarded by the ancient Greeks as the holiest of sites. (The second motto, by the way, was "Nothing in excess," emphasizing the importance of moderation and balance in one's life.)

Prior to Socrates, the conventional interpretation of "Know yourself" was something along these lines: "Know your place, your status, and your duties in society, and be true to them. Do not try to usurp a position in society not yours by right of birth or divine command." Undoubtedly, the greatest impact of such an interpretation was felt by those in possession of neither political power nor wealth—that is, the "underclass," which in ancient Athens meant everyone except a relatively small group of aristocratic families. Thus, if you were, for example, a blacksmith or a farmer, much less a slave, you were expected to be the best blacksmith, farmer, or slave that you could be—but no more.

One of Socrates' greatest and most enduring legacies, one for which he ultimately gave his life, was to fundamentally transform the meaning of "Know yourself" by turning it *inward*. In other words, when Socrates advised his fellow Athenians—the aristocrats, more often than not—to examine their lives, to "know themselves," he was exhorting them to give far less time and attention to external circumstances like social status and wealth and to give much more time and attention to the things that matter most: internal goals, like wisdom, truth, and ethical character. As Socrates himself expressed the point in defense of his teachings:

> I will not cease from philosophy ["love of wisdom" in the ancient Greek language] and from exhorting you, and declaring the truth to every one of you I meet, saying in the words I am accustomed to use: "My good friend, are you not embarrassed by caring for money and how to get as much of it as you can, and for fame and

> reputation, and not caring or taking thought for wisdom and truth and for your soul [or your 'character'], and how to make it as good as possible?" . . . I go about doing nothing else but urging you, young and old alike, not to care for your bodies or for money sooner than, or as much as, for your soul [or your "character"], and how to make it as good as you can.

Like all truly great teachers of things most important, Socrates continually challenged others to look in the mirror and ask themselves penetrating questions about the improvement of their "souls," their personal characters. Master teachers like Socrates force us to ask ourselves these kinds of questions: "If I do not care or strive to be a better human being, then what does that say about the condition of my life, much less the condition of my personal character?" "What happens if our society as a whole ceases to care about the improvement of its collective soul?" "Isn't improving ourselves 'internally' what, in largest measure, our lives are supposed to be about in the first place?"

Whether or not some, most, or all people are ethically complacent or whether they care about and strive for internal self-improvement are questions we will set aside throughout this discussion, if for no other reason than we probably shouldn't presume to answer such questions for others anyway. But we can and should ask these questions and answer them for ourselves. So let's take Socrates' admonitions seriously and begin our own process of looking in the mirror by asking and answering honestly the following questions:

Have I become complacent about improving my personal character?

Am I so consumed in my daily life with other pursuits and goals that I end up devoting little or no time and thought to the betterment of my personal character?

How much time and energy do I spend trying to enhance my looks or my popularity or my bank account in comparison to the time and energy I spend trying to improve my personal character?

Have I perhaps developed an attitude of "Oh well, I'm too set in my ways now," or "I'm content with the way I am, faults and all—so I won't bother trying to improve any more"?

Do I recognize, or have I taken the time to recognize, how much room for improvement there actually is within my own personal character?

To what extent do I really care about taking personal ethics to heart and striving to become a better person?

To what extent am I willing to devote the time, thought, and energy necessary to improve my personal character?

In all honesty and humility, I have never met a person who didn't (or couldn't) respond with something like "Wow, that one really hits home with me" to one or more of these questions. More than one of them has certainly hit home with me. Even though I regularly write, teach, and speak about issues of ethics and personal character, I nonetheless have to remind myself continually, amid the hustle and bustle of my own professional and personal responsibilities, to look in the mirror and ask myself some of these questions. I'll be the first to tell you that those of us who might be good at "talking the talk" need to take the time to make sure that we are "walking the walk" as much as anyone else.

What about you?

Not surprisingly, one of the first and not-so-pleasant steps you and I must take when looking in the mirror is to identify and acknowledge those specific things in our own personal characters that require improvement—in other words, our *faults* and *weaknesses* of character. Truth is, there can be no meaningful improvement without addressing that part of ourselves, which is what we will begin doing in the next chapter.

For now, I'll leave you with four pertinent and powerful aphorisms. The first two are from the pens of two renowned nineteenth-century Scottish writers, Thomas Carlyle and Robert Louis Stevenson, respectively; the last two are from the pen of the seventeenth-century Spanish Jesuit priest Baltasar Gracian.

The greatest of faults is to be conscious of none.

You cannot run away from weakness; you must some time fight it out or perish; and if that be so, why not now, and where you stand?

Know your major defect. Every talent is balanced by a fault, and if you give in to it, it will govern you like a tyrant. You can begin to overthrow it by paying heed to it: begin to conquer it by identifying it. Pay it the same attention as those who reproach you for it. To master yourself, you must reflect upon yourself. Once this imperfection has surrendered, all others will follow.

Know yourself: your character, intellect, judgment, and emotions. You cannot master yourself if you do not understand yourself. There are mirrors for the face, but the only mirror for the spirit is wise self-reflection. And when you stop caring about your outer image, try to emend and improve the inner one. In order to undertake matters wisely, gauge your prudence and perspicacity. Judge how well you measure up to a challenge. Plumb your depths, weigh your resources.

CHAPTER THREE

Character is what you are in the dark.

Dwight Moody

In the ancient Greek world, long before Heraclitus, Socrates, and Aristotle lived, a myth was told about a shepherd who served the king of Lydia (an ancient country of Asia Minor, in present-day western Turkey). One day, in the midst of a severe thunderstorm, the shepherd watched in dismay as a violent earthquake ripped open the ground and created an enormous chasm where he was tending sheep.

Overcome by awe as well as sheer curiosity, he climbed down into the chasm. Among many other marvelous objects, he saw a hollow bronze horse of disproportionately large size. Climbing through one of the horse's several window-like openings, the shepherd caught sight of a giant-sized human corpse, which was wearing nothing but a ring of gold on one of its fingers. He pulled the ring from the corpse's hand, put it on his own, and climbed out of the chasm.

Several days later, during a regular monthly meeting in which the royal shepherds reported to the king on the state of his flocks, the shepherd inadvertently turned the ring upside down on his finger. Upon doing so, he immediately became invisible, and his fellow shepherds sitting around him continued talking as if he had stepped out of the meeting. Dumbfounded by what had just happened, the shepherd turned the ring back over and immediately became visible again.

After testing it several more times, the shepherd came to realize the ring's power of invisibility. In the days following this discovery, the shepherd took full advantage of the ring's power. As we might say now, he "went crazy" in a very calculated and unethical fashion: he schemed to become one of the king's personal liaisons, he committed adultery with the king's wife, and, with her help, he murdered the king and took over the Lydian kingdom.

The ancient Greek philosopher Plato (Socrates' most famous student and Aristotle's intellectual mentor) recounts this myth in his best-known work, the *Republic*, a dialogue-form treatise exploring the nature of justice. Early on in the work, where the myth is described, Plato's two principal characters, his teacher Socrates and his brother Glaucon, are engaged in a debate on the specific question of why someone should be ethical.

In the course of the debate, Glaucon uses the myth to raise the following provocative question: If human beings could do whatever they wanted, without any consequence of being seen by others, what would human beings be like and what would they do?

The way in which we would answer this question reveals a great deal about the way in which we view basic human nature—whether we view human beings by nature as good or bad or a mixture of both. However, I have not shared the myth with you to delve into this deep and controversial philosophical issue.

(In case you're curious about Glaucon and Socrates' respective views, here's a thumbnail sketch: In sharp contrast to Socrates and Plato, Glaucon believes that people would not be ethical if they could get away with being unethical, for two reasons: first, human beings are naturally predisposed to be selfish and unethical; second, there are no good, overarching reasons to be ethical apart from human laws. Socrates and Plato, like most of us, believe there are very good reasons to be ethical, even if in possession of a magic ring of invisibility. Whether human beings would in fact be ethical under those circumstances is the crucial question that we're going to be asking in this discussion.)

Controversial issues about human nature aside, I have retold the myth about the shepherd's ring for two very practical aims. The first is to continue turning our self-examining eyes directly toward the proverbial mirror. At the same time, I want to establish for our discussion a helpful and easy-to-remember working conception of character.

Consider, then, that in an important sense all of us do possess an invisibility ring—those times when we can do things while no one's looking or we're by ourselves ("in the dark"). Now ask yourself this rephrasing of Glaucon's question:

If I could do whatever I wanted, without consequence of being seen by others, what would I be like and what would I do?

Both personal and professional experience have taught me, however, that leaving the question this way is still too abstract and thereby too comfortable for our purposes. What we need to do is put the question in terms more concrete, for what we're ultimately seeking—if we genuinely desire to improve ourselves—is truth and perspective, not comfort.

So to ensure that we're being as truthful and realistic as possible in this self-examination process, let's ask ourselves pointed questions like these:

> If I could do whatever I wanted, without any consequence of being seen by others, would I tend to be:
>
> Kind or unkind?
>
> Honest or dishonest?
>
> Trustworthy or untrustworthy?
>
> Respectful or disrespectful?
>
> Faithful or unfaithful?
>
> Self-controlled or not self-controlled?
>
> Responsible or irresponsible?

This line of questioning is valuable, if not essential, for it encourages us to think in terms of what exactly it is that determines what we are "in the dark." The answer? *Our habits of character.* Our personal bundle of good and not-so-good habits of character.

As you will see, this notion of habits of character will play—must play—a prominent and crucial role throughout our discussion. When we, in our adulthood, take the time to look in the mirror and ask ourselves questions about what we would tend to be in a certain situation, we're not primarily asking what we would consciously choose to be in that particular situation. We're primarily asking what, in light of our past experiences (including our upbringing) and past choices, as well as our present day-to-day behavioral patterns, we would "by nature" be in that situation.

We're asking what it would be our habit to be.

The classical idea of *habits of character,* as we are and will be using it, is far richer than today's common, simplistic concept of habits as mindless, and typically undesirable, behaviors. Indeed, the classical idea of habits of character is virtually identical to what has often been described in the Judeo-Christian religious tradition as "habits of the heart"—a wonderful, holistic notion that is meant to capture all at once one's intellectual, volitional, emotional, and spiritual capacities, particularly as they are collectively and concretely manifested in the customary actions of our day-to-day lives. This is precisely how I would like for us to think of habits of character: those ways in which we would typically be inclined to think, feel, and act on a daily basis.

As a contemporary moral philosopher has put this critical point:

> There is, for better or worse, a predictability in our lives, a stability of choice, an ingrained disposition to act in

one way rather than another. We are disposed, because of the actions we have already performed, to perform similar actions in the future. This is what is meant by habit: a disposition to perform acts of a certain kind.

That we are disposed to act in a certain way does not mean, of course, that we will always or necessarily act in that certain way or that we will always or necessarily act according to what is our habit. We are *not* robots. Nor are we, ethically speaking, like Pavlov's dogs, always and uncontrollably manifesting the same conditioned reflex to a given stimulus: We may not be able to control the way in which our mouths water every time we see or smell freshly baked homemade bread (I can't!), but we certainly can control our tendencies to be impatient, dishonest, disrespectful—if we set our minds to it and work at it. Just as importantly, we're not mere lumps of clay, always passively and helplessly being shaped by external forces.

We *do* have the capacity to act contrary to our habits, contrary to those ways in which we are disposed to act. I may be impatient by nature, but this does not mean that I will or must always act impatiently. Or I may be honest as a matter of habit, but I am still capable of being dishonest. And it's worth noting in this regard that, if every once in a while I do act contrary to these habits—in other words, from time to time I do act patiently or dishonestly—I would nonetheless remain, as a matter of habit, both an impatient and honest person.

To have habits of character simply though profoundly means that we are disposed to act in certain ways in certain situations. While we do have the capacity to act contrary to our personal habits, the sobering reality is that *most of the time most of us will act in a manner consistent with our habits.* And that's why we must take our habits seriously when we each aim to become a better person.

Now, habits can be either good or bad. In the ethical sense of the term, as we are and will be using it, habits have traditionally been called either virtues (good habits) or vices (bad habits). It is our habits, our personal assortment of virtues and vices, that primarily constitute our character and thereby determine what we are in the dark. Aristotle, echoing a view held by virtually all cultures from time immemorial, captured the essence of character as habit when he remarked succinctly:

We are what we repeatedly do.

Common sense would suggest that being in possession of a magic invisibility ring would only serve to magnify or intensify what we have repeatedly done in the past—that is, our dominant habits, both good and bad.

Which of your habits would most likely be magnified or intensified?

As many people have told me, and as I can personally attest, taking the time to ponder the possibilities can be both extremely enlightening and sobering.

Late one evening, for example, while talking informally with a group of friends and acquaintances about this sort of self-reflective process (someone had asked me about the latest book I was writing—this one), I half playfully, half seriously challenged the entire group, asking whether they would be willing to describe, in front of everyone, one each of their most notable good habits and bad habits of character. After everyone seemed to consent, I started out by offering, "On the positive side, I think I am a person who's consistently true to his word. But, on the negative side, let's just say that in many everyday situations, at work and at home, I could use a lot more patience—and I mean a lot."

The responses following mine were so honest, sobering, and moving—some from individuals who were essentially strangers to most in attendance—that I quickly grabbed a piece of paper to scribble several of them down. The first brave soul to respond after me, a woman in her forties, said, "Being sensitive to other people's feelings comes very easy to me, but—don't laugh—I have a very bad habit of whining when I don't get my way." Everyone laughed, including the woman herself.

Another person, a woman in her mid-thirties, said, "I would say that I am a very honest person, but, to tell you the truth, I am too quick to judge people before I really get to know them." No one laughed, but more than a few people nodded their heads, signaling that they understood the woman's bad habit all too well.

A man in his late thirties, a good friend of mine, replied, "I don't think anyone would disagree that I'm a very disciplined person." Then he confessed, "But, with all the really bad stuff going on in politics and in our society generally, I've noticed lately that I'm in a really bad habit of being cynical about and distrusting just about everything and everybody." Most of us nodded empathetically, and a long, silent pause ensued.

The silence was broken by a wonderful woman in her forties—considered to be a "saint" by those of us who knew her—when she offered this personal insight about herself: "I seem to have an endless amount of love and compassion to give other people—I give all the credit to God—but, after all these years, I'm still trying to learn, slowly but surely, how to think before I speak. My lightning-speed mouth still gets me into a lot of trouble!" Everyone broke into laughter.

Toward the end of the conversation, a shy, soft-spoken man in his late twenties, who clearly wasn't all that anxious to participate in this particular discussion, courageously shared these words: "Kindness is probably my greatest virtue; I can be nice and polite to people without even thinking about it or working at it." His voice began to quiver and his eyes welled up with tears. "But—I can't believe I'm going to say this—very recently I learned the hard way just how easy and natural it was for me to be deceitful. My habit of deceitfulness was so bad that it finally caught up with me. I had worked as a supervisor in a large department store for two and a half years, and, for the last year, almost every week or so, I had gotten in the habit of stealing electronic items from my department. Well, I got caught, and I got fired. I'm just lucky they didn't press charges against me. Worst thing was, the deceit and stealing got to the point where I didn't even think about what I was doing—I just did it."

As you can imagine, the rest of us sat there in stunned silence. We weren't shocked because we had learned that a "vicious thief" was sitting among us. (On the contrary, I can now vouch that this young gentleman is an otherwise good and decent person, one I would be proud to have as an employee, his mistakes—crimes—notwithstanding.) We were shocked more than anything else because of his naked honesty and vulnerability. He wasn't simply admitting what it was his bad habit to *be*. He was admitting in very concrete terms what had become his bad habit to *do*.

Taking this courageous young man's lead, we can take our own self-reflective process at least one step further in the direction of concreteness and practicality. Our original question was "If I could do whatever I wanted, without consequence of being seen by others, what would I be like and what would I do?" We have already started inquiring about what we would be, but what about what we might actually do? Allowing me to frame the question as pointedly and challengingly as possible, ask yourself, for example, these questions:

> If I could do whatever I wanted, without consequence of being seen by others, would I:
>
> Shoplift items from a store?
>
> Cheat on an exam?
>
> Illegally copy computer software?
>
> Invade someone's privacy to spy on him/her?
>
> Steal from my employer?
>
> Cheat on my tax return?

Betray a friend or loved one?

Give false information on a resume or loan application?

Harm someone I don't like?

Or would I possess the virtues, such as honesty, respect, and self-discipline, necessary to refrain from these actions?

To the extent that you ask and give honest answers to these types of soul-searching questions, as I will encourage you to do throughout our discussion, you can begin to get a clearer picture of your own personal character. You will see a clearer picture of your strengths and weaknesses of character, of your virtues and your vices. And you will see a clearer picture of those specific ways in which you are truly a good—or truly a not-so-good—person.

As you can see, I am using character in the profoundly ethical sense of what you, as an adult human being, are deep down in your essence: the *real* you, stripped away of all that is transient, superficial, and exterior. "Character is what you are in the dark," as the nineteenth-century lay evangelist Moody expressed, and it is revealed most tellingly in the things you do—especially in those things you do consistently, habitually, or *character*istically, on a day-to-day basis.

CHAPTER FOUR

The final forming of a person's character lies in their own hands.

Anne Frank

The title to this chapter is a profound sentiment about character formation. It is a favorite quote for many people, including myself, especially considering the horrific circumstances under which these words were penned and the extraordinary, uncommon character of Anne Frank.

At the age of fifteen, when most of us were hanging out with our high school friends, talking—or at least fantasizing—about our first "real" date or first kiss, Anne was writing these powerful words into her diary, at the start of her third year of hiding out from the Nazis, under the constant fear of death.

To give you a better appreciation of the meaning of Anne's words about taking responsibility for one's own character, here is more of that particular day's diary entry:

> I have one outstanding trait in my character, which must strike anyone who knows me for any length of time, and that is my knowledge of myself. I can watch myself and my actions, just like an outsider. The Anne of everyday I can face entirely without prejudice, without making excuses for her, and watch what's good and what's bad about her. This "self-consciousness" haunts me, and every

time I open my mouth I know as soon as I've spoken whether "that ought to have been different" or "that was right as it was." There are so many things about myself that I condemn; I couldn't begin to name them all. I understand more and more how true Daddy's words were when he said: "All children must look after their own upbringing." Parents can only give good advice or put them on the right paths, but the final forming of a person's character lies in their own hands.

This profound passage is in fact part of what, unknown to her at the time, would be Anne's third-to-last journal entry, dated Saturday, July 15, 1944. Only two more entries would follow: one six days later, on Friday, July 21, and one seventeen days later, on Tuesday, August 1.

On Friday, August 4, 1944, only three weeks after Anne wrote the passage quoted above, the Nazi police found and raided the hiding place that had given Anne, her family, and four friends uneasy refuge for just over two years. All eight occupants of the hiding place were arrested and sent to German and Dutch concentration camps. Seven months later, in March 1945, Anne died of typhus in a concentration camp in northern Germany.

Anne's "final forming" passage eloquently makes the vital point that concluded the first chapter: You and you alone ultimately determine your final character. As an adult, the responsibility for becoming a good person is ultimately yours and nobody else's. Not his, not hers, not theirs—just yours.

Although very young, Anne possessed remarkable insight into what is perhaps the first greatest challenge to becoming a person of excellent character: taking full responsibility for what kind of person you are now and for what kind of person you will become. This has much to do with the ethical "self-consciousness" Anne wrote of, that minute-to-minute, day-to-day awareness of whether your behavior "ought to have been different" or "was right as it was." It's a matter of continually looking in the mirror—the moral mirror, so to speak—"entirely without prejudice, without making excuses for [yourself], and watch[ing] what's good and bad about [yourself]."

No one has ever said this process is easy. In fact, it is painstakingly difficult for most of us. Have you ever asked yourself why that is? Why continually being a good person and doing the right thing can be so difficult?

While there are certainly no magical, one-size-fits-all answers in this regard, I can offer this basic and practical insight: difficulties that arise in being a good person and doing the right thing most often reside in us. In *me*. In *my own* personal character.

The difficulty is typically due to something occurring deep in ourselves that takes the form of intense, one-on-one struggles between the following:

What I *ought* to do

vs.

What I *want* to do

or

How I *feel* at the moment

or

What I would *like* to happen

or

What I *fear* might happen to me

However, here again is an example of a level of description that runs the risk of leaving an important point too abstract for it to meaningfully impact our thinking, much less our behavior. Giving these internal struggles a bit more everyday concreteness, then, consider what they can actually end up looking—and *feeling*—like:

I should play fairly.
vs.
I want to win no matter what it takes, at all costs.

I shouldn't break my promise to keep this secret.
vs.
Right now I would love to tell my friends this secret.

I ought to tell the truth about what happened.
vs.
I'm afraid of what'll happen if I tell the truth.

I shouldn't copy someone else's copyrighted software.
vs.
I really want this software—besides, it's so *easy* to copy.

I know I should apologize to her for my actions.
vs.
The last thing I feel like doing is apologizing to her.

I shouldn't break this rule or law.

vs.

I want to keep up with the competition,
so I'd better break this rule or law.

Now think about it. What's ultimately going to decide the outcome of these internal struggles? What's ultimately going to make the difference in determining whether you do the right thing or not?

The determining factor is nothing less than the strengths—and weaknesses—of your character.

That's the hard truth of the matter. We can talk at great length about the pressures, about the temptations, about how he did this and she did that, about how everyone else is doing it, about how they were going to do this and they weren't going to do that, about how stressed out we were, and about any number of other things. But even if all these are very *true*, in the end they may be very beside the point when it comes to being a good person and doing what is right.

If we're honest with ourselves, we'll see that these sorts of responses in defense of our actions often amount to not much more than a handful of self-serving excuses. (Please don't think I'm pointing any fingers here. Believe me, I've got my own bag of ready-to-use excuses and rationalizations that I'm continually attempting to overcome.)

Take a careful look one more time at the list of internal struggles above. Notice that I didn't include in the list items such as this:

I shouldn't break this rule or law.

vs.

Everyone else is breaking this rule or law.

Can you see why? The reason is telling: We don't typically break rules or laws because everyone else is breaking them. Nor can we ever really blame anyone else for the rules or laws we break. We break rules or laws most often because of something we *want*. Because we want to succeed. Or because we want to gain an advantage over someone else. Or because we want the convenience or the luxury. Or because we want to win. Or because we want to be accepted. Or because we want to be famous. Or because we want money or some material possession. We do it usually for something we want. And that means it's still going to be an issue for which each personal character is ultimately and solely responsible.

Thus, when it comes to wrong behavior, such as breaking rules or laws, the real struggle is not between you and everyone else—or anyone else, for that matter. The real struggle is still an internal one between what you should do and what you want; in other words, between

I should follow the rules and laws.

vs.

I want something so badly that
I will break the rules and laws.

The same goes for virtually any kind of unethical conduct.

As a strong rule of thumb, what everyone else is doing will be quite irrelevant when it comes to doing what is right. It doesn't really matter what your friends and relatives are doing or saying; what your neighbors are doing or saying; what your coworkers are doing or saying; what your bosses are doing or saying; what politicians are doing or saying; what the media are doing or saying; or what practically anyone is doing or saying.

When all is said and done, no one can force you to do something against your will that you know to be wrong.

Therefore, I am ultimately responsible for my character as well as the actions that I allow to flow from my character.

CHAPTER FIVE

Character is higher than intellect.

Ralph Waldo Emerson

The title for this chapter was part of a lecture given by Emerson in 1837 on the campus of Harvard University. Emerson boldly used this five-word assertion to conclude a keynote lecture he had been asked to give at a meeting of the Phi Beta Kappa national honor society.

Standing before his distinguished academic audience, the renowned American writer and philosopher had been expressing his concerns about the limits of knowledge and a college's overarching educational goals. In particular, Emerson was worried (in 1837, mind you) that institutions of higher learning were in danger of focusing so narrowly on the goal of "book knowledge" that they would lose sight altogether of an equally important aim: helping students use their newly acquired ideas and theories to become good, decent, and responsible human beings.

Over 150 years later, while writing about similar concerns, the eminent Harvard psychiatrist Robert Coles would tell a poignant story about one of his students who was struggling to come to terms with the truth of Emerson's words. The student, named Marian, was a sophomore majoring in philosophy. She came to Coles' office one day to confide in him how badly—how *unethically*—many of her fellow students continued to treat her.

In great anguish, she poured her heart out to the professor: Coming from a Midwestern, working-class family, Marian was cleaning the rooms of her classmates to work her way through Harvard; she described how these high-IQ, "best and brightest" classmates not only did not have the decency to ever say "please" or "thank you" but did not hesitate to be outright rude and crude toward her.

Marian told Professor Coles about being blatantly propositioned a number of times by an exceptionally bright premed student who was already an accomplished journalist. "That guy gets all A's," she said. "He tells people he's in Group I [the top academic category at Harvard]. I've taken two moral reasoning courses with him, and I'm sure he's gotten A's in both of them—and look how he behaves with me, and I'm sure with others."

After a long pause at the end of the two-hour conversation, as if giving her professor time to soak it all in, she asked pointedly and unnervingly: "I've been taking all these philosophy courses, and we talk about what's true, what's important, what's *good.* Well, how do you teach people to *be* good? What's the point of *knowing* good, if you don't keep trying to *become* a good person?" (Coles' emphasis).

Finally, as Marian stood up and proceeded to walk toward the door, she left Professor Coles with this provocative aside: "I wonder whether Emerson was just being 'smart' in that lecture he gave here. I wonder if he ever had any ideas about what to *do* about what was worrying him—or did he think he'd done enough because he'd spelled the problem out to those Harvard professors?"

"She was pointedly reminding me," Professor Coles shares pensively, "that she hadn't forgotten my repeated references to [Emerson's speech at Harvard], to the emphasis its author . . . placed on character, the distinction he made between it and intellect. She was implying that even such a clarification, such an insistence, could all too readily become an aspect of the very problem Emerson was discussing—the intellect at work, analyzing its relationship to the lived life of conduct (character), with no apparent acknowledgment of (unease with respect to) the double irony of it all! The irony that the study of philosophy, say, even moral philosophy or moral reasoning, doesn't by any means necessarily prompt in either the teacher or the student a daily enacted goodness; and the further irony that a discussion of that very irony can prove equally sterile, in the sense that yet again one is being clever—with no apparent consequences, so far as one's everyday actions go."

Not too many days after that pensive conversation, Professor Coles tells us lamentingly, the disheartened Marian left Harvard for good. But her haunting questions certainly remain—not just for Coles and Harvard but for all of us.

Setting aside the more complex issue of higher education's responsibility to shape character in addition to broadening intellect (after all, the focus of our discussion here is on taking responsibility for our own personal character), let's think about Marian's soul-searching question, which asked:

What's the point of knowing good, if you
don't keep trying to become a good person?

Marian undoubtedly asked this specific question rhetorically, meaning she didn't expect an answer because the answer was so obvious. And, of course, it is. When all is said and done, the only legitimate answer one can give to this question is something like, "There is no point." What other meaningful point could there possibly be? From the perspective of any individual person, *the one and only point of knowing good is becoming good.*

Despite its rhetorical nature, however, the question is well worth pondering, for it implicitly speaks volumes to us about why being a good person is a matter of what you are—of personal character—more than anything else, even more than what you know.

Lest there be any misunderstanding, I should be quick to emphasize that my point (and certainly Emerson's) is in no way meant to detract from the value of knowledge. Quite the contrary, what you know is very important, and increasing your knowledge can certainly help you become a better person.

Nonetheless, as Marian's unenviable experience with some of her Harvard classmates clearly illustrates, this fundamental truth always looms large: Knowing what is right and good is no guarantee that you will do what is right and good. Indeed, whether you do what you know to be right and good will ultimately be determined by the strengths and weaknesses of your personal character and not by your IQ, not by your standardized test scores, not by your academic degrees, and not by any ethical theory or moral reasoning courses that you may have taken and passed with flying colors.

Just because one knows a great deal about anything at all, even ethical theory and moral reasoning, does not make one a good person. As I am thankful to my parents for often emphasizing, *being smart does not necessarily mean being good.* We can take it a step further: Knowledge without character—without virtues such as honesty, self-control, responsibility, and compassion—is worthless at best and evil at worst. Or, as President Theodore Roosevelt famously expressed it, "To educate a person in mind and not in morals is to educate a menace to society."

The upshot here is that the all-important
connecting link between
knowing right and good
and
doing right and good
will always be
having the character to do what is right and good.

On a practical level—and by "practical" I mean on a real-world, day-to-day basis—this point simply can't be stressed enough.

Why?

Because most of the time in our everyday lives, we do in fact know what is the right and good thing to do. Not all the time, to be sure, but most of the time. And we may not always know precisely or completely, but we usually know at least generally.

Although these days we commonly talk, hear, or read about "ethical dilemmas"—those difficult situations in which we truly are perplexed as to the right course of action—it is crucial to recognize that these dilemmas, for most of us, represent the exception and not the rule in our lives. In other words, it's not as though most of us are confronted on a daily basis with complex and controversial dilemmas—like mind-boggling and heart-wrenching life and death issues—that are beyond our immediate ethical comprehension. What typically is the rule in our daily lives is not a matter of knowing what is right and good but having the character to do what is right and good.

This is not to minimize the importance and seriousness of genuine ethical dilemmas. Make no mistake, you and I will face complex situations in which we struggle rationally and emotionally to determine what's right or best, ethically speaking. And, for a variety of not-so-simple reasons, some people will face more of these situations than others. At times we may have to make a decision on the spur of the moment, when we really don't have enough time to sort out all the pros and cons. At other times, with a little advice from a friend or family member, or with plenty of time to think the whole thing over on our own, we can make the most ethically expedient decision possible.

But ethical dilemmas as such are not normally a day-to-day or even a week-to-week circumstance for most of us. The primary difficulties that we face in our daily quests to do what is right and good are typically not difficulties of knowing but of doing, not of knowledge but of personal character.

A prominent professor of education has made the following point in his influential book treating the moral education of the young:

> A great deal of a child's moral life—or an adult's, for that matter—is not made up of dilemmas at all. Most of our "moral decisions" have to do with temptations to do things we know we shouldn't do or temptations to avoid doing things we know we should do. A temptation to steal money from her mother's purse is a more common problem for the average girl than deciding whether or not to turn in a friend who is shoplifting.

Likewise, for adults, the temptation to call in sick to work when perfectly healthy—that is, to blatantly lie, not to mention steal time and money from one's employer—is certainly a more common problem than deciding whether it is morally justifiable to kill an intruder who has broken into one's house.

Take once again the mistreatment of Marian. It wasn't as if her disrespectful fellow students didn't know that they shouldn't be rude and crude toward her. And it certainly wasn't as if the exceptionally bright premed student didn't know that blatantly propositioning a woman (repeatedly) was demeaning, unethical behavior.

Consider these telling results from a recent comprehensive national survey titled "Report Card on American Integrity":

- Twenty-four percent of college students and nearly 10 percent of adults not in school admitted that they would lie to get or keep a job.
- Sixty-one percent of college students and 26 percent of adults not in school admitted that they had lied to a parent in the last year.
- Virtually *all* of these adults put together agreed—on the very same survey!—that "honesty is the best policy" (over 97 percent) and that "it is dishonest to intentionally misrepresent a fact or to deliberately cause another person to believe something that is not true" (approximately 95 percent).

Statistics like these, and especially the personal experiences of our everyday lives, clearly reveal that many, if not most, of the problems precipitating bad behaviors are not problems of the head, so to speak, but of the heart and will—of character.

Recall our discussion about internal struggles from Chapter 4. To the extent that we face difficult ethical struggles in our normal, day-to-day lives, the vast majority of the time we will be dealing with internal struggles of personal character of this type:

What I *know* I *ought* to do

vs.

What I *want* to do

A more concrete example is the following:

I *know* I should treat her respectfully.

vs.

Because I want to feel superior and be in control,
I'll say or do whatever it takes to put her in her place.

The ultimate "arbiter" of these internal struggles is nothing less than the constitution of your personal character, the choices of which are continually displayed in your daily actions—good or bad—or, in other words, are embodied in your daily responses to the question:

Do I have the character to do what is right and good?

CHAPTER SIX

Excellence is habit.

Aristotle

Because the primary ethical challenge of our day-to-day lives is not usually a matter of knowing what is right and good but of having the character to do what is right and good, the all-important, destiny-determining question for us will largely be one of *how* to develop character that does what is right and good.

A very useful and simple, though certainly not simplistic, answer to this question can be found in Aristotle's *Nichomachean Ethics*—the Western world's philosophical *locus classicus* (i.e., the classic exposition) on the nature and development of excellence in ethical character.

Aristotle writes in the second major section of the *Ethics:*

> *Ethical excellence comes about as a result of habit.*

He elaborates on this foundational point by comparing the development of virtues—excellent habits of ethical character—to the development of excellent skills in crafts or the arts:

> We acquire virtues by first exercising them, as in the case of the arts. Whatever we learn to do, we learn by actually

> doing it: for example, we become builders by building, and harp players by playing the harp. In the same way, we become just by doing just acts, self-controlled by doing self-controlled acts, brave by doing brave acts.

Aristotle's observation is, in and of itself, probably not very revealing or surprising to you. One obviously needs to spend a great deal of time and energy practicing the craft of carpentry if one desires to become an excellent carpenter. Likewise, one should devote countless hours to practicing a musical instrument if one's goal is to become a first-rate performer of that instrument.

The ancient Greek poet Hesiod expressed this idea several hundred years before Aristotle:

> In front of excellence the immortal gods have put sweat, and long and steep is the way to it.

So too have innumerable other accomplished individuals throughout human history expressed the same basic truth asserted by Aristotle. In more recent times, the world-renowned pianist Arthur Rubinstein (1887–1982) once observed about his musical mastery:

> If I omit practice one day, I notice it;
> if two days, my friends notice it;
> if three days, the public notices it.

Driving home the very same kind of point in reference to his own extraordinary accomplishments in the sports world, legendary pro football coach Vincent Lombardi (1913–1970) once remarked:

> We must pay a price for success. It's like anything worthwhile. It has a price. You have to pay the price to win and you have to pay the price to get to the point where success is possible. Most important, you must pay the price to stay there. Success is not a "sometimes" thing. In other words, you don't do what is right once in a while, but all the time. Success is a habit. Winning is a habit.

Hesiod, Rubinstein, and Lombardi (and countless others) all capture in their respective sentiments the largely commonsense truth about achieving excellence described generally by Aristotle. Call it the First Universal Principle of Excellence: To become excellent at any particular art or skill requires a lot of hard work, a lot of sweat, a lot of practice.

What may not be so obvious, however, and what can actually be very revealing and helpful to us, is Aristotle's insight that this principle applies equally to the pursuit of excellence of ethical character: *Becoming a person of excellent ethical character is precisely analogous to becoming an excellent carpenter, musician, or athlete.* As we quoted Aristotle before, "In the same way, we become just by doing just acts, self-controlled by doing self-controlled acts, brave by doing brave acts."

In other words, ethical excellence, just like musical or athletic excellence or excellence of any kind, will in largest measure be a result of developing good habits—habits that can only be achieved through ceaseless determination, hard work, and practice. The upshot: If you want to develop good habits of ethical character (virtues) such as honesty and respect, then you must literally practice being honest and respectful. (To give you a fuller, working grasp of this point, I will offer a few true-to-life, concrete examples in Chapter 9.)

We can gain an even greater appreciation for the analogy between developing excellence of ethical character and developing musical, artistic, or athletic excellence if we ask the general question, as Aristotle does: What exactly does it mean to be excellent at something? It certainly doesn't mean doing something well only occasionally, Aristotle reminds us. While we might say of a particular musician, "She gave an excellent performance last night," we wouldn't usually describe her as an excellent musician if that performance, unlike several prior mediocre performances, happened to be her only laudable one to date. She might fairly and accurately be described as a decent or capable musician, but we would typically reserve the term "excellent" for a musician who consistently, perhaps even invariably, performs excellently.

And that's the key to being truly excellent at something: knowing how to do something so well that you are capable of doing it well again and again, so consistently well that it becomes "second nature" to you. That's precisely why pianists who yearn to perform on an Arthur Rubinstein level of musical excellence will spend countless hours practicing scales and arpeggios, and that's why aspiring athletes run, lift, swim, throw, catch, swing, shoot, or kick thousands and thousands of times to have the opportunity to compete in world-class sports (and perhaps do so under the master tutelage of a legendary coach such as Vince Lombardi). The object is to do something excellently not merely once in a while but all the time, effortlessly and unthinkingly.

Think about it like this: In the same way that we admire (and perhaps try to imitate) the athletic excellence of a Michael Jordan, the artistic excellence of a Meryl Streep, or the musical excellence of a Luciano Pavarotti, we likewise admire (and hopefully try to imitate) those people near and dear to us who have excellent ethical character—our ethical role models. Individuals such as Jordan, Streep, and Pavarotti all perform their respective arts extremely well, in a natural and consistent manner. That's the key: doing what is excellent naturally and consistently. In the case of our ethical role models, one of the greatest reasons we hold them in such high regard is that they invariably do the right and good thing with such ease and consistency. Not unlike the way in which excellence flows naturally from deep within the world's maestros, virtue just flows naturally and consistently from the character of ethical role models, or, as we also call such outstanding individuals, "moral exemplars."

Consider Bruce and Ruth, the wonderful couple from whom I recently purchased a used Dodge Caravan. They had taken excellent care of the five-year-old vehicle, and Bruce and Ruth had made every effort to ensure the van's integrity and safety prior to selling it—including, at their own unnecessary expense, a mechanical inspection the day I bought it. Despite all their efforts, an incredible thing happened: the van's transmission completely failed on my way home just minutes after completing the transaction.

Keep in mind that Bruce and Ruth were total strangers to me before I responded to their ad in the paper. Here's what happened next: More than a little upset and frustrated, I called Bruce from a pay phone near the place where I had been stranded just off the freeway. He immediately came to my aid, waiting with me for about an hour until a tow truck arrived. After the van had been towed to a convenient gas station in my neighborhood, Bruce unhesitatingly paid for the (very expensive) tow, and then he took me home.

Upon reaching my house, Bruce, obviously as disheartened as I was, promptly offered to return my check. Talk about an incredibly strong sense of integrity and personal responsibility. He was under no legal obligation whatsoever to give me my money back, especially since I had officially bought the van "as is." What struck me most about Bruce's response was his immediate and palpable concern not only for my feelings but also for his own deep-seated sense of what is *right*. In other words, the excellence of character he showed was obviously ingrained in his personal character, as evidenced by the way he so naturally, effortlessly, and immediately acted responsibly, respectfully, and generously on my behalf. (Incidentally, we ended up splitting the expenses for a new transmission, and I am exceedingly happy with my "new" van, thanks to Bruce and Ruth's uncommon integrity.)

When thinking of people I know well and who naturally and consistently do the right thing, I can't help but think—if you don't mind my saying so—of my wife, Jeannine. In all of my presentations or lectures on this topic, I invariably find myself invoking examples of Jeannine's absolutely unwavering and automatic sense of honesty, a virtue undoubtedly instilled in her early on by her mother, Roberta, another paragon of truthfulness. In this respect and others, Jeannine is certainly a role model to me. In situations where I might be tempted to cut corners with the truth, bend the truth, or finesse the truth to my own (selfish) advantage, Jeannine seems virtually incapable of telling even the most inconspicuous little white lie. (And it's a mark of her humility that she will be more than a little embarrassed when she discovers that I have shared this anecdote about her in this book!)

Before becoming a full-time mom and homemaker, Jeannine worked for nine years in the ferociously competitive, high-stakes business of mortgage banking. She worked for a large, national mortgage banker, and her specific role was that of account executive—a sales representative who dealt directly and solely with mortgage brokers who themselves were trying to get the best loan package for their particular clients. Almost daily, sad to say, Jeannine would be asked by certain brokers to help them attain loan approval on a loan package that contained, at best, ethically questionable information and, at worst, blatantly false information—the latter of which would obviously constitute the crime of fraud. (My intent here certainly isn't to make unfair, sweeping judgments about brokers; as my wife would be the first to say, a majority of brokers in the industry are people of integrity.)

Despite the reality that in many cases no one would be the wiser for the dubious or false information and despite the fact that it would certainly mean substantially more money in her pocket, Jeannine (as I have seen or heard her do many times) would unfailingly and instantaneously react with dismay and disgust that anyone would have the nerve to ask her to be less than honest. "You've got to be kidding, right?" or "Let me get this straight, you're actually asking me to break the law?" or, in some extreme cases, "I am now going to hang up" were Jeannine's very typical, habitual responses. Technically speaking, she is *capable* of being less than honest, of course, but her disposition to tell the truth is so strong, so relentlessly and virtuously powerful, that the temptation to be anything but completely honest typically does not even arise for her—as it certainly would for me.

With examples such as these, of exemplary individuals who naturally and consistently exhibit excellent ethical habits in their daily lives, notice that we also have the key to resolving those difficult, internal struggles between *what I ought to do* and *what I want to do*. We saw in Chapter 4 that the resolution to these internal struggles must be found in the strength and determination of our personal character; now we have a specific way of dealing with them. By developing strong habits of ethical character, we find that many of these internal struggles cease to be struggles at all, for we possess the strong—or dominant—natural tendencies to do what we ought to do.

(My use of "dominant" can be a bit misleading, especially from an Aristotelian perspective, so it's worth clarifying. To speak as if *what I ought to do* should always "dominate" *what I want to do* can suggest that these two choices are always at odds with each other. While this particular issue can be somewhat controversial depending on one's view of basic human nature, common sense would tell us, as Aristotle does, that *what I ought to do* and *what I want to do* need not and will not always be in conflict. To claim otherwise would mean that none of us ever desires to do what is right and good, which, of course, is absurd.)

As Aristotle himself concludes, becoming a person of excellent ethical character will always, *must* always, involve developing good ethical habits (virtues) to such an extent that they become ingrained in our character. To such an extent that we won't merely occasionally do what is honest, fair, self-controlled, and respectful, for example, but will do so naturally and consistently in our day-to-day lives. To such an extent that *what I ought to do* and *what I want to do* often become the same thing. Indeed, in Aristotle's way of thinking, if you say no to some unethical behavior, it's not merely because you shouldn't but because you wouldn't; and if you say yes to an action that is ethically appropriate, it's not merely because you should but because you would. Doing what is right and good is not merely something you do but something you *are*—your personal character.

CHAPTER SEVEN

Whatever is true, whatever is noble, whatever is right, whatever is pure, whatever is lovely, whatever is admirable, if anything is excellent or praiseworthy, fix your thoughts on such things.

Paul, the Apostle (Phillipians 4:8)

Call it the Second Universal Principle of Excellence: One does not become excellent at something primarily by focusing on and avoiding what is wrong and bad but by focusing on and pursuing what is right and good.

This principle holds true for the Michael Jordans, Meryl Streeps, and Luciano Pavarottis of the world, and it holds equally true for you and me in our respective quests to develop excellence of personal character. Specifically, for our character-building purposes, the principle can be put this way: *Our primary goal as moral beings is not just to say no to vice but to say yes to virtue—as a matter of heartfelt habit.*

The distinction between saying "no" to vice and saying "yes" to virtue helps explain why Paul, in his role as moral and spiritual mentor, didn't say to the Christians at the ancient Greek city of Phillipi something like this: "Whatever is false, whatever is dishonorable, whatever is wrong, whatever is impure, whatever is ugly, whatever is disreputable, if anything is immoral or contemptible, avoid thinking about such things." To be sure, Paul's New Testament writings do include admonitions of this negative sort, concerning why and how to eschew vice. But like all great moral and spiritual leaders, he primarily focused his counsel on the positives—why and how to pursue whatever is "excellent or praiseworthy."

The reason is simple, though vital. Excellence and praiseworthiness are not the mere nonexistence of wrong and bad things; they are real and independent moral qualities in and of themselves. "Virtue," the early twentieth-century English author G. K. Chesterton once noted, "is not the absence of vices or the avoidance of moral dangers; virtue is a vivid and separate thing."

I realize this language may sound rather esoteric, but the practical, destiny-determining importance of this distinction truly is hard to overstate. And, I would hasten to add, it applies to the vexing social problems of our day as much as to issues of personal character: Excellence is never achieved by primarily—much less exclusively—focusing on the elimination of what is wrong and bad. On the contrary, to achieve excellence, our focus, our aim, and our practice—all of our mental, emotional, and spiritual energies—must be directed primarily toward the pursuit of what is right and good.

Do you feel the force of this point? Do you see what I'm driving at?

Consider the profound difference between, say, on the one hand, making it our day-to-day goal to "just say no" to such things as drugs, crime, prejudice, incivility, and sexual exploitation, and, on the other hand, making it our day-to-day goal to "just say yes" to such things as good health, integrity, impartiality, civility, and respect.

The two goals are not mutually exclusive. Very often, they are mutually supportive. And certainly, "Just Say No" programs—like the recent "Just Say No to Drugs" campaign—represent noble and (lamentably) necessary community-based efforts.

But the two goals are fundamentally different, and, more important, they are not equal, neither theoretically nor practically speaking. The extent to which your personal character and my personal character, as well as the character of our society in general, will enduringly be changed for the better will in large measure depend on the extent to which the pursuit of virtue, and not the renunciation of vice, prevails as our supreme, character-building objective.

To use one of my favorite metaphors, attaining ethical excellence is like growing an excellent garden: It depends on the cultivation of beautiful flowers and not on the eradication of weeds as its top gardening priority. A contemporary moral philosopher has memorably painted the image with these words:

> Trying to become virtuous merely by excluding vice . . . is as unrealistic as trying to cultivate roses solely by eliminating weeds. After clearing the garden of weeds, one must still plant seeds or cuttings and nurture their growth; otherwise, the weeds simply return. The best way to exclude vices is to crowd them out with the presence of strong virtues.

The imagery is vivid and powerfully commonsensical. Think about the responses, not to mention facial expressions, you would receive upon asking people with "green thumbs" (skilled gardeners or farmers) whether pulling weeds is their chief agricultural aim. Their responses might be like these: "Are you joking?" "Is this a trick question?" "Have you noticed that I'm called a 'farmer' or a 'bearer of fruits' and not a 'weeder'?"

Similarly, how much sense would it make for us, as caretakers of our own ethical "gardens," to think and act as if eliminating vices were our number one goal? By definition—that is, by Nature, by Grand Design—we are called moral beings, not "immorality-eliminating beings." (Let ridiculous notions have ridiculous names!)

Allow me to illustrate the point further by way of my young children's bookshelves. Among the many other wonderful books now in their possession, Nicholas and Gabriella have a complete set of the Help Me Be Good series from Grolier Enterprises. There are twenty-nine books in the series, all of which are designed to focus on specific ways to facilitate the character development of children. Take a moment to read carefully through this complete list of titles:

Being a Bad Sport
Being Bossy
Being Bullied
Being Careless
Being Destructive
Being Forgetful

Being Greedy
Being Lazy
Being Mean
Being Messy
Being Rude
Being Selfish
Being Wasteful
Breaking Promises
Cheating
Complaining
Disobeying
Fighting
Gossiping
Interrupting
Lying
Overdoing It
Showing Off
Snooping
Stealing
Tattling
Teasing
Throwing Tantrums
Whining

What strikes you about this list? Its most obvious characteristic is that all the titles, without exception, describe negative behaviors or bad traits of character—vices, as we have been using the term. In fact, after reading all twenty-nine books, it becomes clear that this series focuses less on helping children to be good and focuses more on helping children understand why not to be bad. Its emphasis is more on identifying and pulling weeds than on planting and nurturing flowers. (To be fair to the series, I should point out that each book typically contains a page or so encouraging children in a positive sense, for example: "You should treat other people the way you want to be treated." Nonetheless, all of the books, as the titles suggest, are unmistakably negative in their force and point.)

Please don't misunderstand me here. I am in no way implying that because its focus is primarily on why not to be bad, this series of books has no character-building value. I believe very much the contrary: Weeds definitely need to be identified and eliminated, especially for young and impressionable children, and my own children continue to benefit from reading the clear and colorfully illustrated Help Me Be Good books.

My point is that in its present form, such a series is *incomplete* from the standpoint of ethics, morality, and character education. Again, saying no to vice is not the same thing as saying yes to virtue. Pulling weeds can certainly help us cultivate flowers, but pulling weeds is importantly not the same thing as cultivating flowers.

Rather than focusing on pulling weeds, we must focus on planting and feeding flowers—virtues—of the sort I have tried to illustrate with the following comparative list:

Virtues ("Flowers")	**Vices ("Weeds")**
Being a good sport	Being a bad sport
Being polite	Being bossy
Being friendly	Being bullied
Being careful	Being careless
Being constructive	Being destructive
Being mindful	Being forgetful
Being generous	Being greedy
Being industrious	Being lazy
Being nice	Being mean
Being neat	Being messy
Being respectful	Being rude
Being selfless	Being selfish
Being responsible	Being wasteful
Keeping promises	Breaking promises
Playing by the rules	Cheating
Complimenting	Complaining
Obeying	Disobeying
Cooperating	Fighting
Praising	Gossiping
Listening	Interrupting
Being honest	Lying
Being balanced	Overdoing it
Being humble	Showing off
Respecting others' privacy	Snooping
Respecting others' property	Stealing
Minding one's business	Tattling
Caring	Teasing
Having self-control	Throwing tantrums
Being responsible	Whining

While reading through these lists, I hope you were reminded—as I was while composing the virtues list—that these are not merely children's virtues and vices. They are *our* virtues and vices. As adults we may use different terms to describe them (although most of the time we do not), but they are the very same virtues and vices. A child who throws tantrums and an adult who loses his or her temper are both contending with the same vice—on different levels of maturity and experience, to be sure, but it is the same basic vice nonetheless. Likewise, a child who tends to be obedient and responsible and an adult who, as a matter of habit, respects authority and is a dutiful citizen are both exhibiting the same basic virtues.

Thus, recalling the profound truth captured by the title of Robert Fulghum's best-selling 1986 book, *All I Really Need to Know I Learned in Kindergarten*, we can appreciate how my example from children's literature does not so much represent a temporary excursion into the moral education of the young as it represents another leg of our trek into the heart of *adult* moral education.

You can and should ask yourself which of the virtues and vices listed previously are ingrained parts of your own personal character. In addition, I would encourage you now to reflect on whether the personal-growth aims of your daily life, in general and to date, are best described as a conscious yes to the virtues listed above *or* as a conscious no to the vices listed above. (There is obviously another alternative, which represents the worst-case scenario: One could simply not be giving any conscious thought or effort to becoming a better person.)

I would also encourage you to consider, for your character's sake—your *destiny's* sake—the overarching theme of this chapter: Although consciously saying no to the vices listed previously is both admirable and necessary, becoming a person of excellent character can never be achieved on the basis of avoiding or eliminating vice. It can only be achieved by means of the sustained, heartfelt pursuit and promotion of what is intrinsically right and good—like those virtues listed previously.

Fixing our thoughts on planting and cultivating flowers—virtues—that's what it's really all about.

An afterthought: One of the easiest decisions I had to make while writing this book was whether or not to try composing a "definitive list" of virtues. I have no trouble believing there may be such a list, and I have no trouble with the many individuals throughout history who have understandably and laudably attempted to identify a complete set of virtues. At the same time, I have absolutely no trouble believing that I cannot—and should not—presume to take on such a task myself. (In all candor, part of me suspects that such a task is tantamount to an attempt to read the mind of God—from whom, I believe, all virtue originates.)

If anything—classicist that I am—I believe that the Western tradition's paradigm of seven foundational virtues is difficult to improve upon: Faith, Hope, and Love, often called the three theological virtues; and Prudence (practical wisdom), Justice (fairness), Fortitude (moral strength/courage), and Temperance (moderation/balance), often called the four cardinal or human virtues. However—realist that I am—I recognize, for example, that these days we seldom speak of prudence, fortitude, and temperance (which explains why I felt compelled to put synonyms for these terms in parentheses). I also recognize that the claim "I have the definitive list of virtues!" will understandably create more problems than solutions. Such presumptuous claims can even work *against* the cultivation of virtue.

One of the main reasons I have offered the list of virtues, or "flowers," is because lists of so-called children's virtues are typically very concrete and practical, which is often what we adults need, given our tendencies to over-complicate or rationalize what can be quite elementary. Remember, our primary aim is to have a positive and practical impact in other people's lives as well as our own. In service of that goal, a good rule of thumb is to create a list of basic virtues that makes sense to a kindergartner. Whether it's an official corporate code of ethics or a scribbled piece of paper taped to your refrigerator, the virtues highlighted on that list should concretely engage the hearts and minds of the young as well as the "old." Food for thought.

CHAPTER EIGHT

To enjoy the things we ought to enjoy . . . has the greatest bearing on excellence of character.

Aristotle

Thus far, we've collected insights, both ancient and modern, concerning the nature and development of excellent character. Toward the goal of taking to heart these insights, ask yourself now:

Am I a person who has the personal character to do what is right and good, to do what is virtuous?

More specifically, ask yourself these questions:

Can I truly be described as a person of honesty, fairness, self-control, respect, trustworthiness, patience, and so forth?

How can I even tell whether I actually have one or more of these virtues?

Even with such practical, getting-to-the-heart-of-the-matter questions as these, the high-minded philosopher Aristotle offers us some help. In the *Nichomachean Ethics,* he presents what I call Aristotle's "virtue test": an informal and easy-to-remember checklist of criteria for determining whether or not a particular virtue is truly an ingrained part of one's character. (Aristotle himself never explicitly calls this a test or checklist, but what he describes functions precisely like one.) The test consists of five relatively straightforward criteria, with each criterion representing an essential part of what it takes to possess genuine virtues of ethical character.

As I describe Aristotle's virtue test, keep in mind three important qualifications. First, I do not consider, as Aristotle himself did not consider, his test to be either airtight or foolproof. It certainly doesn't explain everything. And, as Aristotle makes very clear, what we are delving into—one's personal character—is not something that lends itself to precise, scientific measurement. Nonetheless, when kept in proper perspective, Aristotle's test can be a useful tool for those who genuinely desire to get the most out of a serious look in the mirror.

Second, Aristotle's virtue test is an *ideal* test for virtue. In other words, his test describes the ideal conditions by which one could be said to have a particular virtue completely or perfectly ingrained in one's character. It could probably go without saying that most if not all of us are far from having every virtue (or even one virtue) completely or perfectly ingrained in our character. But that should just serve as a reminder to us of the importance of continually looking in the mirror. A test such as Aristotle's has necessary and practical value in that it is an ideal standard to which we can aspire.

Third, as the name I have given it implies, the primary focus of Aristotle's test is on virtue, not vice. While the five criteria of the test, by implication, can and will undoubtedly tell us something about our vices, Aristotle's emphasis—not unlike the general emphasis of this book—is on studying, developing, and strengthening virtues. Why? For the same basic reason emphasized in Chapter 7: The most effective way, and sometimes the *only* way, to rid ourselves of bad habits of character is by proactively studying, developing, and strengthening good ones.

Now, let's explore Aristotle's virtue test.

In the same section of the *Ethics* in which Aristotle draws a comparison between developing excellence of ethical character and developing excellent skills in crafts or the arts (which we discuss in Chapter 6), he describes the following five criteria for determining whether one has a given virtue:

1. You must know what you are doing.

This especially means you must know that what you are doing is virtuous. You must realize that what you are doing is in fact honest or respectful or fair and so on.

2. You must choose to do it of your own free will.

In other words, you must make a conscious decision to do what is virtuous, without anyone forcing you to do what is virtuous.

3. You must do it for its own sake.

That is, your motive must be to do what is virtuous simply because it is virtuous, and not because it might benefit you socially, politically, or financially or it might help you avoid pain, punishment, or embarrassment, and so forth.

4. It must flow naturally and consistently from your character rather than being an isolated incident.

This is the very same point of Aristotle's that I emphasized in Chapter 6.

5. You must enjoy doing it.

In other words, when we act ethically, we should characteristically feel good about, even derive pleasure from, doing what is right and good. This particular criterion is probably the most arguable of the five. I believe it represents a very noble standard worth striving for, but I do not believe—as Aristotle seems to—that a person who doesn't enjoy doing the right thing in a given situation is somehow less virtuous. Would any of us want to argue that moral exemplars such as Jesus and Gandhi and Socrates are less virtuous because they may not have enjoyed sacrificing their lives for what was right and good?

The best way to use this virtue test, Aristotle suggests, is to apply the five criteria to particular actions in our day-to-day lives. To give you a sample of how the application works, let's imagine the following scenario about a basically decent, hardworking, and churchgoing fellow named Ned:

> Ned is in the grocery store, at the checkout counter, and he has just handed the cashier a $10 bill to pay for groceries worth $6.75. The cashier gives Ned $13.25 in change, mistakenly thinking that he had paid with a $20 bill. With full knowledge of the cashier's mistake, Ned unhesitatingly pockets the $13.25 and walks out of the

store, feeling kind of lucky and self-satisfied for having "made" an extra $10.

Now, we could end our scenario right now, with Ned keeping—in other words, *stealing*—the money, in which case it would be obvious that he lacks the virtue of honesty. Instead, let's extend the scenario as follows:

> After thinking the whole thing over at home for a few hours, Ned begins to feel guilty. Despite feeling a bit sorry for himself for having to give up some "easy" money, that same day he ends up returning the ill-gotten $10 to its rightful owner, the grocery store.

This particular scenario focuses primarily on the virtue of honesty, that is, on the extent to which honesty is truly an ingrained part of Ned's personal character. The fact that Ned acted dishonestly on the front end of the situation obviously demonstrates that honesty is far from being completely ingrained in his character. He did, however, eventually act honestly by returning the money, so we just as obviously shouldn't conclude that dishonesty is completely ingrained in his character.

This is no small point. Quite the contrary, the point is foundational, for it illustrates a universal truth well worth remembering throughout our discussion: None of us are perfect in ethical character, and most of us are far from perfect. Thus, when it comes to having particular virtues like honesty, self-control, or respect, most of us (just like the basically decent, hardworking, and churchgoing Ned) will not be either *completely* honest or dishonest, completely self-controlled or not self-controlled, or completely respectful or disrespectful. We will find ourselves somewhere in between—closer perhaps to completely honest, self-controlled, and respectful, but nonetheless at a place with plenty of room for improvement.

Aristotle's virtue test is valuable in the way it helps reveal just how much room for improvement does in fact exist in our personal character. Notice the insights we discover when we apply Aristotle's five criteria to Ned's situation (keep in mind that we're focusing primarily on his eventual act of honesty, not his initial act of dishonesty):

1. *You must know what you are doing.* Ned clearly knew that returning the money was the honest thing to do, just as clearly as he knew that taking the money was the dishonest thing to do. (Ned's situation illustrates, by the way, one of the central points of our discussion in Chapter 5: On a day-to-day basis, we usually know what is the right and good thing to do.)

2. *You must choose to do it of your own free will.* To Ned's credit, no one compelled him to do what was honest (no one had compelled him to do what was dishonest, either). It was his own conscience that prompted him to finally make the right decision and return the money.

3. *You must do it for its own sake.* Here we must do a bit of speculation, if for no other reason than only Ned (and God) could ultimately reveal to us the true motives of his heart (just as only you and I can

ultimately know the motives for our own individual actions). If Ned returned the money simply as a matter of principle—because it was the honest thing to do—then he did meet this criterion. However, if he returned the money, for instance, for fear that he might get caught or might suffer embarrassment, then he did not in fact fulfill this criterion. In other words, while Ned eventually did do the honest thing, there would still be room for improvement within his personal character because he didn't do the honest thing with the best and highest of motives.

4. *It must flow naturally and consistently from your character, rather than being an isolated incident.* Ned obviously didn't do the right thing naturally. If the virtue of honesty had been truly ingrained in his character, he wouldn't have knowingly taken the money in the first place. He did eventually return the money, but he had to think it over a great deal, which suggests that he was experiencing one of those intense, internal struggles between what he *ought to do* and what he *wanted to do.*

5. *You must enjoy doing it.* As I have described the scenario, we can't conclude that Ned felt very good about returning the money. Not only was it rather difficult for him to return the $10, but when he did do so he felt a touch of self-pity for having to give up such "easy" cash.

In this analysis, I do not want to undermine or in any way belittle the fact that Ned eventually did the right thing, the honest thing. His honest action is praiseworthy—not completely, to be sure, but praiseworthy nonetheless. With Aristotle's insightful help, what I have tried to emphasize is that like the basically decent Ned, most of us have plenty of room to improve when it comes to being a truly good person, a person of excellent ethical character—even in situations in which we basically (or eventually) do the right thing.

Aristotle's virtue test can go a long way in helping us get a handle on weak areas within, and specific ways to improve, our personal character. Make no mistake, however; his test requires that we be completely honest with ourselves when looking in the mirror and asking about particular actions in our daily lives:

1. Did I know that this was the right and good thing to do?

2. Did I choose to do it of my own free will?

3. Did I do it for its own sake?

4. Did it flow naturally and consistently from my character?

5. Did I feel good about doing it?

CHAPTER NINE

No one who desires to become good will become good unless he does good things.

Aristotle

From the don't-mince-words-just-say-it-like-it-is column: When someone says, "You can't teach an old dog new tricks" in defense of his or her own character flaws and weaknesses, it is an insult not just to human beings, but to dogs as well.

It's insulting for one simple reason: It's false.

From the standpoint of improving our personal character and striving for ethical excellence, this old and worn-out cliché amounts to nothing more than a fatalistic, self-defeating poison or an excuse similar to "I'm too busy to deal with it"—or both.

That's why it's important for us always to bear in mind a crucial point emphasized in Chapter 1:

> *You and I, as human beings, have the innate capacity to determine who we are or what we want to be, or should be, over and above what we are "by nature."*

This self-determining capacity does not disappear simply because we, as adults, are now "set in our ways." That's the reality, which the "old dog" cliché and others like it belie.

Set in our ways—in other words, set in our *habits*—you and I may indeed be. But this does not change the fact that some of our ways may be far from virtuous, and it certainly does not change the fact that you and I have the innate ability to *change* our ways, our habits, when appropriate or necessary.

No one has said, of course, that changing our habits of personal character comes easily. In truth, the process can be very difficult.

That's precisely why Aristotle says in the *Nichomachean Ethics*, at the very beginning of his discussion on developing excellence of character: "The habits we form from childhood make no small difference, but rather they make all the difference." He knew all too well, just as you and I know, that old habits can die hard.

Notice, however, what he says later on, at the conclusion of his virtue test discussion:

> No one who desires to become good will become good unless he does good things. Yet most men do not do these; instead, they resort to merely talking and theorizing about them and think that by doing so they will become virtuous, thus behaving somewhat like patients who listen to their doctors attentively but do none of the things they are told to do. And just as these patients will not cure their body by behaving in this way, so those who merely talk and theorize about becoming good will not better their soul.

Aristotle believes that even as adults we have the potential—indeed, the responsibility—to improve our "soul." Improving our soul will invariably entail changing some of our ways, teaching ourselves "new tricks," and not merely talking about but *doing* good things. Literally practicing at doing good things until we do good things as a matter of practice—that, in a nutshell, is what changing for the better is all about.

Changing our ways may be difficult, but it's never impossible. To think otherwise is to deny our humanity. As the nineteenth-century novelist George Eliot remarks in her classic work *Middlemarch:* "Character is not cut in marble; it is not something solid and unalterable. It is something living and changing."

A recent in-depth study reported on twenty-three Americans who have provided extraordinary moral leadership. This study helps expose the lie perpetuated by the "old dog" cliché, and at the same time it helpfully qualifies Aristotle's remark that the habits we form in childhood make *all* the difference. The researchers' point, which Aristotle would not deny, is that good childhood habits of character do not guarantee good adult habits of character (recall Anne Frank's important sentiment, "The final forming of a person's character lies in their own hands"). Consider the following passage from the opening chapter of the study:

> How is this rare quality of [extraordinary moral] dedication developed and maintained? What, if anything, does it have to do with early experience? In asking these questions, we start with the realization that many people raised in secure, warm, and ordered family environments do not acquire this quality. We also start with the belief

> that some unusually dedicated people come from backgrounds quite the opposite. For all these reasons, we are skeptical about analyses that reduce extraordinary moral commitment either to social factors such as family background or to personal ones such as a tendency to have close relationships. We are in fact skeptical about the role of *any* early experience in determining the course of moral commitment. One of the characteristics of highly moral people is their ability to learn from their experience all throughout life. . . .

Throughout their study, the researchers discovered that many of the twenty-three outstanding ethical role models did not even begin their morally extraordinary endeavors until their late forties, an observation that should prompt us to throw out the "old dog" cliché in favor of another old, yet much more constructive, one: "Where there's a will, there's a way."

Here, incidentally, is a notable point at which, as Aristotle recognizes, the analogy between developing excellence of character and developing musical, artistic, or athletic excellence no longer holds. All the willing and determination in the world won't help most of us achieve the athletic excellence of a Michael Jordan, the artistic excellence of a Meryl Streep, or the musical excellence of a Luciano Pavarotti. Most of us simply do not possess the innate abilities necessary to ascend to the upper echelons of athletic, artistic, or musical excellence.

But *all* of us, as human beings, do possess the innate abilities necessary to achieve excellence of ethical character—excellence in the sense of improving our personal character to the point where we can do right and good things naturally and consistently.

We certainly can't expect this improvement to happen overnight. In most cases, it will happen little by little, day by day, habit by habit.

What I would like to do now is offer a couple of true-to-life examples of how this habit-by-habit process of character improvement works, or at least how it *can* work. The first story is a brief and personal—even confessional—anecdote from my own life; the second, lengthier story describes a process of character transformation in the life of one of my former students.

Before I became engaged to my wife, Jeannine—I am more than a little embarrassed to admit this publicly—I never wore a seat belt when in a car. As the driver or as a passenger, it made no difference; I neither liked nor wanted to wear one. (Notice the classic conflict between *what I want to do* and *what I ought to do*.) For close to fifteen years, most of these years in clear violation of the law, I simply, stubbornly, refused to wear a seat belt.

Now, we could analyze my foolish behavior from any number of angles, but all of these angles would ultimately lead us to one significant fact: a flaw in my personal character. What else could it have been? It wasn't as if I didn't know that wearing my seat belt was the right thing to do. And it wasn't as if someone else was forcibly preventing me from wearing it. The fact of the matter is that I had developed a very bad habit, one which not only violated common sense but the law of the land as well.

In short, I had a bad habit of doing the wrong thing.

It was Jeannine who helped me get in the habit of doing the right thing. I'll never forget the not-so-playful glance she gave me when, only a few short days after I had proposed to her, she said to me in passing as we drove to meet friends for dinner, "If you want me to marry you, you'd better start wearing your seat belt." While on that occasion I did put on my seat belt, Jeannine read me like a book: She knew that I had put it on primarily for her, and, more to the point, she knew my bad habit was so ingrained that even if I were serious about changing my ways (which I was beginning to be), I wouldn't automatically and consistently start strapping myself in.

The next morning, when I got in my car to leave for work, I found a three-inch-square piece of yellow paper from a Post-it notepad stuck to my dashboard, with a short message:

R,

I love you very much.
Please remember your seat belt.
I want you to be with me 4-ever.

J

Jeannine, wise and practical-thinking woman that she is, made me promise on the phone later that morning that

I would not remove the note until, in her words, "you begin putting on your seat belt without thinking about it, every time you get into your car."

The note remained in place for just over a year. At the end of that time, I was finally doing the right thing, "by nature."

Now to appreciate as much as possible the practical implications of Aristotle's central insight that we acquire good habits by doing good things repeatedly, consider that, on average, four times a day, seven days a week, and for over twelve months, I couldn't help but see Jeannine's note every time I got behind the wheel of my car. That adds up to well over 1,400 times that I consciously thought about and put on my seat belt *before* I began putting it on naturally and consistently, as a matter of habit. And that, as Aristotle would exhort us, realistically illustrates the kind of commitment and practice often required to develop good ethical habits, much less to change bad habits into good ones.

Thanks in large measure to my wife, my best "friend" in the Aristotelian sense, an old dog had been taught a new—and virtuous—trick.

"I have come to the realization, Professor Gough," she said with tearful eyes, "that lying has become second nature to me. I tell little white lies as easily and calmly as breathing."

These were the first words that came out of her mouth after she took a seat in my office.

I'll call her Emma—a bright and amiable student of mine, who, at the time, was in her late twenties.

To say that I was surprised by Emma's words would be a gross understatement. I was shocked—not simply because of what she said but also because she was saying it to me. After all, I'm neither a therapist nor a man of the cloth by training; I'm a teacher, a university professor. To say the least, it's not often that a college student will speak with such self-incriminating candor to his or her professor.

Emma was close to finishing her second class with me; the class was an ethics course. In this course, Emma, her fellow students, and I had recently finished a series of readings and class discussions, philosophical and practical in nature, revolving around themes of ethical character not unlike those in this book. Several selections from Aristotle's *Nichomachean Ethics* were among the required readings.

Sitting in my office that afternoon, Emma explained how these readings and class discussions had contributed to her sudden *mea culpa:*

> What hit me the hardest were our discussions about habits, and especially about how our personal habits can really say the most about the kind of person we are. I started thinking about my own habits, but especially about my habit of telling people things that aren't true. The more I thought about it, the more it made me feel sick to my stomach, because I realized that my habit of lying was so bad that it might actually be the most distinguishing feature of my personal character—even if

known only to me. How can I call myself a good person if I'm a liar?

I must confess that I was relieved she had asked this poignant question rhetorically, because I wasn't prepared to answer it, at least not *for her*. Emma and a few other students had pressed this sort of question in class, asking whether someone could be called "a good person" if that someone naturally and consistently did things, for example, that were dishonest, disrespectful, or unfair. The noble, even if not completely satisfactory, conclusion reached by the class was that in most cases, unless talking in the abstract, this type of question would be best answered according to the heart of each self-examining individual.

After regaining her composure, Emma continued:

> I can't exactly pinpoint when this habit began. I think it started way back in high school. All I know for sure is that for the past several years I've told so many lies to friends and family members and employers and teachers that I now lie without even thinking about it. That's what really bothers me the most—that I lie as if it were really my nature to lie. I do it every week, sometimes daily. As best as I can figure, I usually tell these lies to make myself look good or simply to cover up for myself, to escape responsibility in some way. But they're usually small lies, so to speak, not big ones.

She didn't elaborate on her distinction between small and big lies. And she didn't offer any examples, except for admitting in passing that she had lied to me at some point, as she had lied to other teachers, about why she had missed an exam or hadn't completed an assignment on time.

We talked for a while longer, especially about what proactive steps she might take to break her habit. Given that Emma would be graduating and thus leaving town in a matter of days, and given that my knowledge of her was quite limited (to classroom interaction only), I was frankly at a loss for words of advice to offer her. I decided the best thing I could do under the circumstances was repeatedly and earnestly assure her that, consistent with what we had read and discussed in class, she could overcome this flaw in her character. When Emma left my office that afternoon, I couldn't help but feel a sense of helplessness, a sense that my words of encouragement were woefully inadequate.

This story, however, has a very happy and inspiring ending. Indeed, what I have recounted thus far about Emma's story is essentially a long introduction to help you more fully appreciate what Emma would share with me during a surprise visit to my office nearly two years later. In the company of her husband, and following a few minutes of small talk, Emma told me that the main reason she wanted to stop by was to have a "follow-up" and to "bring closure" to our conversation of two years earlier.

She explained that upon returning home after graduation, she confided in one of her church's ministers about her habit of lying. In addition to other ethical and spiritual counsel he gave her over a period of weeks, the minister made several practical suggestions—"character exercises," as Emma described them, to help her continually keep the virtue of truthfulness in her mind's eye.

He encouraged her, for example, to memorize and think daily about a few key verses of Scripture, including the one from the book of Phillipians that serves as the title of Chapter 7: "Whatever is true, whatever is noble, whatever is right, whatever is pure, whatever is lovely, whatever is admirable, if anything is excellent or praiseworthy, fix your thoughts on such things."

The minister also suggested that Emma try to get in the habit of consciously asking herself before speaking, "Is what I am about to say true?" Since getting into this habit was more difficult than she expected, Emma told me, she took the minister's advice one step further: She wrote little reminder notes about being honest, and she put them in conspicuous places "all over my life," as she described it—in every room of her house, at her office, in her car, on her gym bag, and, especially, she said with emphasis, next to every phone that she used frequently, both at home and at work.

In the last few months, Emma told me with a smile, she had finally begun to sense a real change in her character, a change "from being a habitual liar to being a habitual truth-teller." Her inspiring words represent the best possible way to conclude her story:

> It still amazes me that lying had become so easy for me, and that overcoming it and developing the habit of telling the truth could be such hard work. It's something that I had to think about and work on every single day. I still do. While I hate to think now of how it would have been without the continual support of my husband,

family, friends, and church, I realized early on that no one or nothing was making me lie except myself, and that no one was ultimately going to make me tell the truth except myself. I think a large part of my problem was that too often I simply didn't want to accept responsibility for my actions, and lying became a habitual way for me to ignore my responsibilities.

But I can tell you in all sincerity that with a lot of determination and practice—and, believe me, that's exactly what it is, practice—I'm now at the point where telling the truth is more natural for me than not telling the truth. And I have to tell you it really feels good. I truly feel better about who and what I am as a person, knowing that I can at last in my adult life say to myself and before God that despite other character flaws I continue to work on, "I am an honest person."

A final word of caution: Please do not think that I have offered these two stories on the presumption that they explain everything about improving our character. They certainly don't, as the five criteria of Aristotle's virtue test could easily demonstrate.

They do, however, explain a great deal. At the very least, they help to get us thinking practically about the "how-to" dimensions of improving our personal character. They especially illustrate a vital how-to point that can easily be lost on us during adulthood: *We cannot improve our personal character without a lot of hard work and practice.*

Or, to slightly alter Aristotle's words: To become better, we must diligently work at doing better things.

CHAPTER TEN

Example is not the main thing in life—it is the only thing.

Albert Schweitzer

The simple yet profound sentiment that serves as the title to this chapter was uttered by Schweitzer during the last few hours of his life, on September 4, 1965. How poignantly fitting this must have been to Schweitzer's family, friends, and colleagues.

Distinguished philosopher, theologian, physician, musician, and recipient of the Nobel Peace Prize in 1952, Schweitzer is perhaps best known for his magnanimous work as a medical missionary in French Equatorial Africa. In 1913, having renounced his accomplished careers as a concert organist and pianist as well as a teacher of philosophy, theology, and history, Schweitzer and his wife, Helene, sailed with medical supplies and 2,000 gold marks to the West African country of Gabon. They soon constructed a hospital in the heart of the jungles of Lambaréné, a village on the Ogowe River. By the time of his death, Schweitzer had devoted nearly a half century of his life to the people of Lambaréné.

To those who knew him best—and despite all of his obvious musical and intellectual sophistication, accomplishments, and world renown—Schweitzer's single greatest achievement, true to his own words, was his *example.* The

American writer Norman Cousins, a close friend and long-distance pen pal of Schweitzer's, described it thus:

> The greatness of Schweitzer—indeed, the essence of Schweitzer—was the man as symbol. More important than what he did for others was what others have done because of him and the power of his example. At least half a dozen hospitals in impoverished, remote areas have been established because of him. Wherever the Schweitzer story was known, lives were changed. A manufacturer in the American Midwest read about Schweitzer, sold his farm-implement manufacturing company, and used the money to build a string of medical clinics in the Cameroons. A Japanese professor raised money in Schweitzer's name and started an orphanage. A young German medical school graduate, with no means or resources save a fund of inspiration, went to South America and started a hospital. Tom Dooley and his hospital in Laos became an American legend. A beautiful, talented young Dutch woman learned about Schweitzer and selected a medical career. Six years later she was chief surgeon at the Schweitzer Hospital in Lambaréné. She left later to found a hospital of her own. . . .
>
> Albert Schweitzer is a spiritual immortal. We can be glad that this is so. Each age has need of its saints. A saint becomes a saint when he is claimed by many men as their own, when he awakens in them a desire to know the best that is in them, and the desire to soar morally.

I share this sketch of Schweitzer's life not merely to call attention to his extraordinary example but to emphasize how our own personal examples—famous or not—are in fact "not the main thing" but the "only thing" in life. You do not have to be a Socrates, a Mother Teresa, a Billy Graham, a Martin Luther King Jr., a Mahatma Gandhi, or an Albert Schweitzer to take seriously the degree to which the actions flowing from your own character, for better or worse, can and do powerfully influence those around you. You influence those living with you, working with you, playing with you, watching you, listening to you, and sitting next to you and those whom you would have never dreamed of influencing.

You can especially have an influence on those who are younger and more impressionable than you. With children the question is not *whether* they will learn from someone's example; the question is *from whose* example they will learn. And that example can come from anyone at any point in time.

The oft-heard expression "Values are caught, not taught" involves an exaggeration—values can be and are regularly taught. To say that "values are caught more often than taught" is a more accurate description of the powerful and critical role of example.

No matter who you are and what your circumstances are, the power of your example simply cannot be underestimated. Reflect for a moment on the way in which the following passage has captured the essence of this point in vivid spiritual terms:

> Every life is a profession of faith, and exercises an inevitable and silent influence. As far as it lies in its power, it tends to transform the universe and humanity into its own image. Every man is a center of perpetual radiation like a luminous body; he is, as it were, a beacon which entices a ship upon the rocks if it does not guide it into port. Every man is a priest, even involuntarily; his conduct is an unspoken sermon, which is forever preaching to others. Such is the high importance of example.

This being the case—that our personal conduct always represents an influential, "unspoken sermon"—notice something interesting concerning how we now use, and debate about, the concept of role models. Although the expression "role model" first appeared in the late 1950s, it did not become a household term until the 1980s, especially in connection with professional athletes and other celebrities (see more about celebrities as role models later in this chapter). In classrooms, boardrooms, and living rooms, the question "Who are role models?" is frequently asked and discussed. Are professional athletes role models? Political leaders? Teachers? Parents? Who exactly is a role model? Am I?

On the most basic and most important of levels—the level of ethics and personal character—asking whether *anyone* is a role model is, as logicians would say, tautologous. That is, it's like asking whether water is wet or whether fire is hot. Why? Because as a "center of perpetual radiation," each of us "exercises an inevitable and silent influence" on others—even when we don't intend to do so or don't think we're doing so. In short, we are all role models because we are always setting an example, good or bad.

Even the most recent dictionaries bear out this understanding of role models. Take, for example, the entry in the tenth edition of *Merriam Webster's Collegiate Dictionary*:

> **role model** *n.* A person whose behavior in a particular role is imitated by others.

Given this definition, what person would not be a role model? Who does not occupy a particular role that is imitated by others? There simply is no getting around it: *Each of us is a role model.*

Bear in mind that we are using "role model" as it is most frequently used, in an *ethical* sense. When confusions and debates arise concerning the concept, they often do so because someone has used "role model" in a nonethical sense. For instance, if an aspiring young basketball player says that Michael Jordan is her role model, and by that she is referring solely to his extraordinary athletic abilities on the basketball court, then she is using the term in a nonethical sense. In this sense, very few individuals will turn out to be role models like the indomitable Jordan.

Thus, since it should go without saying that *I am a role model*, the most significant questions to ask ourselves will always be like these:

> Am I being a *good* role model or a *bad* role model?
>
> Am I setting a *good* or *bad* example for others?

Are the actions flowing from my character *positively* or *negatively* impacting those I come in contact with?

No process of looking in the mirror would be complete without asking ourselves these sorts of questions. And when it comes to our example being not just the main thing but the only thing in life, there really are no other consequential questions to ask ourselves beyond these—except for practical, heart-of-the-matter questions like this:

If I am characteristically, as a matter of habit,
setting a less-than-ideal example for others,
then what am I now going to do about it?

Make no mistake, for better or worse you and I are always doing something about our example. Even when we are seemingly doing nothing about it, we are actually doing something, and it's often for the worse, not the better.

One final note: Discussions and debates specifically about celebrities as role models (in the ethical sense, as we have been discussing it) are so prevalent now that I feel compelled to add my two cents' worth. Although this is a book focusing on one's individual personal character, the matter of celebrities as role models is far from irrelevant, especially as our choices in role models can and will contribute to the shaping of our personal character.

The following is an article I was asked to write for *L.A. Parent* magazine in the wake of O. J. Simpson's arrest in the summer of 1994.

Of all the many combinations of letters that a parent can teach a child to create in a warm bowl of alphabet soup, very few were going to be as enjoyable for this sports-fan dad to teach his young son than the combination of "O" and "J."

O.J.

As in O. J. Simpson.

Like countless thousands of people, sports fans and non-sports fans alike, that simple combination of letters had come to symbolize for me things like heroism, discipline, grace, determination, character, success, modesty—in a nutshell, being a role model.

Of course, given the bizarre and tragic melodrama of recent weeks, we're no longer quite sure what "O.J." symbolizes. We're still shuddering to think of the possibilities. But, without a doubt, we can be sure of this: The whole, sordid affair speaks volumes to us, especially as parents, about the very serious business of heroes and role models. There can be no underestimating the power of learning from example, of how profoundly values are caught more often than taught.

Unlike many mothers and fathers, my wife and I feel somewhat fortunate (this time around, at least) that our son, Nicholas, is not even old enough to pronounce "O.J.," let alone struggle with its now-tarnished significance. We certainly haven't envied parents who have had to sort out both for themselves and their disillusioned children why it is that yet another mighty hero has fallen.

However, if this disquietingly tragic pattern of our age continues, and it most likely will, Nicholas will soon enough be asking both us and himself why our heroes and role models so often seem to let us down. That's not always an easy question, intellectually or emotionally, even for parents. When our heroes fall, something inside us and our children falls with them. And whatever that something is, it's been falling like a rock in recent years.

But maybe, just maybe, the greatest object lesson for us to learn from the Simpson tragedy is not so much a matter of our being let down by our heroes and role models as it is a matter of our being more prudent, and more creative, in our selection of heroes and role models. Especially from a parental viewpoint, perhaps the moral of this surreal and sensational story is that we've not always looked in the best places to find someone to look up to, someone to emulate.

When it comes to choosing role models, our culture seems to be suffering from celebrity myopia: It's as if we have tunnel vision, looking only to the high-profile, highly unreal worlds of Hollywood, professional sports, rock 'n' roll—in sum, the world of commercial entertainment. Somewhere along the line in our understandable fascination with celebrities we have bought into the idea that their world, that largely make-believe, escapist world, is a fertile depository of role models.

My point is not that the world of entertainment has no role models. It certainly does. But we'd be kidding ourselves if we didn't accept the fact that choosing from the world of celebrities, in all its superficial glitz and glamour, is very risky business.

Why? At least for one very important reason: Despite all that we read in newspapers and magazines; despite all that we see and hear on television; and despite all those pages we pore over in biographies and autobiographies, we never really know these people. We often like to think we do, but we don't. What we do know, and know well, is primarily veneer. Exterior. Game face, stage face. Persona, not substance. A character, but not character.

For the overwhelming majority of us, our familiarity with celebrities ends at precisely the point where the media-hyped caricature ends. We very seldom ever know what kind of person they really are, what their true character is really like. We don't know them. For all practical purposes, they remain strangers to us and our children.

So perhaps we should backtrack a bit while trying to sort out this unseemly O. J. Simpson affair by asking: Why should we be so quick to choose as our role models individuals whom we really don't know? How surprised or disillusioned should we be when they fall off their pedestal? How much trust and confidence should we—can we—realistically place in a world so far removed from our own?

Precious little, to be sure.

That's why it's imperative for us to encourage our children to look for role models and heroes in places that are considerably less precarious than the world of entertainment. Like home, school, church, Little League, dance class, summer camps, hospitals, and neighborhoods.

In addition to the obvious and important choice of parents as role models, children usually do have a variety of other choices in places very familiar to them. We may have to help them overcome their celebrity myopia (not to mention our own) to help them see other possibilities, but we can do so by regularly and emphatically calling attention to the character, conduct, and accomplishments of exemplary individuals most familiar to them.

So that one day, when our children are asked, "Who has been a role model in your life?" they can respond by saying something like: My mother, unconditional friend. My teacher, cultivator of knowledge and imagination. My doctor, healer of people. My pastor, priest, or rabbi, caretaker of things enduringly true. My Little League coach, model of fair play and sportsmanship. My neighbor, ever the good Samaritan. My ballet instructor, portrayer of grace and discipline. My best friend, keeper of promises and secrets.

Strikingly, all of these examples come from the low-profile, highly real world of authentic familiarity. In sharp contrast to our favorite celebrities, we know these people. Not perfectly, but confidently. Somehow, some way, we must teach our children to see these people, whom we so often overlook and take for granted, as genuine heroes and role models.

We can count on them.

CHAPTER ELEVEN

A man never describes his own character so clearly as when he describes another's.

Jean Paul Richter

On average, how much time and energy do you spend analyzing whether someone else is or isn't being a good example or role model in comparison to the time and energy you spend asking the same question about yourself?

Of the several pointed questions I typically pose to audiences when discussing issues of personal character, this type of question usually generates the most amusing and animated facial expressions: shaking heads, widening eyes, reddening faces, and the like—all of which are usually accompanied by unmistakable sheepish grins. They are amusing, but I certainly sympathize all too well with these expressions.

One memorable time, after posing this question to an unusually responsive audience, I invited a gentleman of about forty years of age named Michael to stand up where he was in the middle of the room. I asked Michael if he could offer an explanation for the group's pronounced reactions to the question as well as his own sudden outburst of laughter and not-so-subtle "Oh, brother!"

"Well," Michael answered, with that sheepish grin on his face, "the question obviously hit home. I would guess that it made more than a few of us feel just a tad bit uncomfortable." (Great laughter ensued as he accentuated "a tad bit" with a raised hand gesture—his thumb tip close to, but not touching, the tip of his index finger.) Before taking his seat, Michael concluded his honest remarks by stating in a more subdued tone of voice, "You might say that some of us have probably gotten into the bad habit of analyzing and criticizing other peoples' characters."

Not nearly as much laughter followed. At this juncture, I was tempted to ask for a show of hands of those who would admit to having this habit, but, given the number of sympathetic looks and nodding heads following Michael's last remark, I decided against it. His candor, even if dressed in lightheartedness, had done more soul-searching good than I could have hoped to accomplish that evening.

There is a related question that I often pose to audiences, especially subsequent to asking the one just mentioned, thanks in large measure to Joseph Telushkin's incisive book, *Words That Hurt, Words That Heal: How to Choose Words Wisely and Well.* The question, which can be found in the opening paragraphs of Telushkin's book, is this: Can you go for twenty-four hours without saying any unkind words about, or to, anybody? Telushkin describes the typical responses he receives, as well as his own insights about them, as follows:

> Invariably, a minority raise their hands signifying yes, some people laugh, while quite a large number call out, "No!"
>
> "All of you who can't answer yes," I respond, "must recognize how serious a problem you have. Because if I

asked you to go for twenty-four hours without drinking liquor, and you said, 'I can't do that,' I'd tell you, 'Then you must recognize that you're an alcoholic.' And if I asked you to go for twenty-four hours without smoking a cigarette, and you said, 'That's impossible,' that would mean that you're addicted to nicotine. Similarly, if you can't go for twenty-four hours without saying unkind words about others, then you've lost control over your tongue."

At this point, I almost always encounter the same objection: "How can you compare the harm done by a bit of gossip or a few unpleasant words to the damage caused by alcohol and smoking?"

Is my point overstated? Think about your own life: Unless you, or someone dear to you, have been the victim of terrible physical violence, chances are the worst pains you have suffered in life have come from words used cruelly—from ego-destroying criticism, excessive anger, sarcasm, public and private humiliation, hurtful nicknames, betrayal of secrets, rumors, and malicious gossip.

Yet—wounded as many of us have been by unfairly spoken words—when you're with friends and the conversation turns to people not present, what aspects of their lives are you and your companions most likely to explore? Is it not their character flaws and the intimate details of their social lives?

Unfortunate but true, Telushkin's point is far from overstated, and it coincides with Michael's concluding remark above: Analyzing and criticizing the personal character and lives of others can become habitual, and *harmfully* habitual in particular. When this sort of behavior has become habitual, it can inflict irrevocable damage not only on those individuals being unfairly criticized and judged (which should go without saying) but potentially on those of us doing the criticizing and judging as well. In the words of the nineteenth-century American theologian Hosea Ballou, "A single bad habit can mar an otherwise faultless character, as an ink-drop soileth the pure white page." Or, in the unpleasantly graphic words of another theologian, the seventeenth-century Spanish Jesuit priest Baltasar Gracian:

> Don't be a blacklist of others' faults. To pay attention to the infamy of others shows that your own fame [or character] is ruined. Some would like to dissimulate, or cleanse, their own blemishes with those of others or to console themselves with them: a consolation of fools. Their breath stinks; they are cesspools of filth. *In these matters, he who digs deepest gets muddiest.* Few escape some fault of their own, either by inheritance or by association. Only when you are little known are your faults unknown. The prudent person doesn't register the defences of others or become a vile, living blacklist. (My emphasis.)

The seriousness and harmfulness of this bad habit of analyzing and criticizing others' character or of "blacklisting" others' faults is difficult to overemphasize, for its result often amounts to nothing less than character assassination (implying irreparable damage to, or even the "death" of, one's good name or reputation). Telushkin illustrates the often unrecognized and harmful power of gratuitous criticism by recounting this well-known tale:

> In a small Eastern European town, a man went through the community slandering the rabbi. One day, feeling suddenly remorseful, he begged the rabbi for forgiveness and offered to undergo any penance to make amends. The rabbi told him to take a feather pillow from his home, cut it open, scatter the feathers to the wind, then return to see him. The man did as he was told, then came to the rabbi and asked, "Am I now forgiven?"
>
> "Almost," came the response. "You just have to do one more thing. Go and gather all the feathers."
>
> "But that's impossible," the man protested. "The wind has already scattered them."
>
> "Precisely," the rabbi answered. "And although you truly wish to correct the evil you have done, it is as impossible to repair the damage done by your words as it is to recover the feathers."

Intimately connected to the fact that criticizing the personal character of others can become a bad and harmful habit in itself is the sobering truth captured by this chapter's title:

What you say about the character of others
reveals a great deal about the constitution and
well-being of your own personal character.

Think about it like this: To the degree that you make, as a matter of habit, genuinely kind and respectful comments about the lives and characters of others, you can be described as a person who possesses the virtues of kindness and respect. Conversely, to the degree that you are in the habit of saying unkind and disrespectful things about others' characters, you can be described as a person who is by nature unkind and disrespectful.

To be sure, and as noted in Chapter 8, many of us are somewhere in the middle of these two ends of the virtue/vice spectrum, somewhere between being completely kind and respectful and completely unkind and disrespectful when talking about others. Even so, virtually all of us have recognizable patterns (habits) of speaking about others, and these patterns—to whatever degree good or bad—can reveal a great deal about the true nature of our own personal characters. (These patterns may be recognizable only to us, but they are nonetheless real and revealing—if, of course, we are honest with ourselves.)

Finally, then, ask yourself these critical questions:

> What is revealed about my character when I talk about the personal character of others?
>
> In particular, what is revealed about my character when I talk about others "in the dark"—behind their backs?
>
> Do I tend to explore and criticize the intimate details of others' lives?
>
> Am I inclined to make a "blacklist" of others' faults?

> Am I in the habit of exploiting the character flaws of others?
>
> Do I tend to make derogatory remarks about others more often than complimentary remarks?

For those of us who may be a little too quick to answer the last four questions with a resounding "No!" Telushkin offers some concrete, cautionary advice:

> [B]efore you assert this as a definite fact, monitor yourself for the next two days. Note on a piece of paper every time you say something negative about someone who is not present. . . . To ensure the test's accuracy, make no effort to change the contents of your conversations throughout the two-day period, and don't try to be kinder than usual in assessing others' character and actions.
>
> Most of us who take this test are unpleasantly surprised.

Yes, we are.

CHAPTER TWELVE

You can follow all the rules and still be unethical.

R. G.

Of all the noble and inspirational aphorisms voiced in the popular and critically acclaimed 1989 motion picture *Dead Poets Society*, there is one in particular, more than any other, that has indelibly etched itself into my pedagogical imagination.

Perhaps unexpectedly, it isn't one of the several citations that the movie draws verbatim from the profound inkwells of past literary masters such as Shakespeare, Tennyson, Whitman, Thoreau, and Blake. While it does play on Thoreau's well-known intent to "suck out all the marrow of life" (a phrase from his classic work *Walden*), the memorable sentiment I have in mind comes from the contemporary inkwell of the movie's screenwriter, Tom Schulman:

Sucking the marrow out of life
doesn't mean choking on the bone.

To remind you (or to inform you, in case you haven't had the pleasure of seeing the film), the movie's action takes place in 1959 at Vermont's Welton Academy, an all-male private prep school rooted deeply in pride, tradition, and discipline. The movie features actor Robin Williams as a passionate English teacher named John Keating who, unlike his more conservative colleagues, stirs up Welton's waters of conformity by using unorthodox teaching methods that explicitly encourage his students to "suck the marrow out of life," to "*carpe diem*" (Latin for "seize the day"), and to "make your lives extraordinary."

Well into the movie's story line, there is an important three-scene sequence, which begins with a scene in the school's auditorium. The school's austere headmaster, Mr. Nolan, has just convened a spur-of-the-moment all-school assembly to determine who has surreptitiously published, in the most recent issue of the school's newspaper, an unauthorized article demanding that female students be admitted to Welton. Just as Mr. Nolan demands that any and all students with knowledge about the article's source stand up and make themselves known, he is interrupted by the sound of a ringing telephone—a telephone sitting in the lap of the sole guilty party, one of Mr. Keating's more impressionable and freewheeling students, the self-christened "Nuanda."

Still seated, Nuanda answers the phone. He says, in a dramatic voice for all to hear, "Hello . . . Yes, he is . . . Just a moment." Then, standing up for the entire assembly to see, he looks toward the headmaster and says sarcastically, "Mr. Nolan, it's for you. It's God. He says we should have girls at Welton."

After a subsequent scene in which Nuanda is scolded and punished by Mr. Nolan, we are taken to a sitting room, where Nuanda, with sunglasses on and slouched in a high-back leather chair, is proudly and sensationally recounting to his friends every detail of his unenviable visit to the headmaster's office. Into the room walks Mr. Keating, and the following exchange ensues:

NUANDA: Mr. Keating.

KEATING: Mr. Dalton, that was a pretty lame stunt you pulled today.

NUANDA: You're siding with Mr. Nolan?! What about *carpe diem* and sucking the marrow out of life?

KEATING: Sucking the marrow out of life doesn't mean choking on the bone. There is a time for daring and a time for caution, and a wise man understands which is called for.

NUANDA: But I thought you'd like that [the prank].

KEATING: No. Your being expelled from school is not daring to me. It's stupid.

This last scene is critical, for it emphatically tempers—that is, puts into proper ethical perspective—the movie's unmistakable emphasis on individual self-expression. Now I'd like to shift from this brief description of a highly entertaining movie to a discussion of issues of deeper and more serious dimensions.

I would probably be remiss here if I wasn't quick to add that certain moments in this sequence, especially the phone-call-from-God scene, are hilariously entertaining. And they are, to be sure. (So, given this admission, please don't take me for an over-analytical, fiber-challenged movie critic for the way I am about to discuss deeper and more serious dimensions of the movie and its message!)

In all seriousness, to best use these scenes in our mirror-looking process, we need to keep in mind that Nuanda's actions, although hilarious on-screen, were clearly *unethical*—

deceit, dishonesty, disloyalty, and blatant rule-breaking were the means to his "hilarious" end. Hence the importance of the picturesque words that Schulman puts into Keating's mouth: *Sucking the marrow out of life doesn't mean choking on the bone.* "Choking on the bone" suggests the point at which we, like Nuanda, can simply go too far with self-interest and self-expression. It represents those times in our lives when we can cross lines that should not be crossed—to the detriment of our own good or society's good.

Now, it is one of the most indisputable and basic facts of human life that lines must be drawn and respected. These lines—*ethical boundaries*—may be explicitly drawn, as in codified laws, or they may be implicitly drawn, such as when we speak of "unwritten rules." Either way, the point still remains: If you and I do not draw and respect lines, we self-destruct. This process of self-destruction may be quick or it may be slow, but it will *be*. On this we can surely depend, whether we're talking about our lives as a whole or about a given domain of our lives: health, love, work, education, finance, athleticism, artistry, and so on.

As important as the necessity of respecting lines is, there is an equally important point concerning the relationship between being ethical and respecting lines. It may, in fact, turn out to be more consequential for our discussion, if for no other reason than it is far less recognized and appreciated:

Taking the personal ethics of our everyday lives seriously is much more than not crossing lines that shouldn't be crossed or not "choking on the bone."

Being ethical—whether being honest, fair, self-disciplined, responsible, or, in general, being a good role model—is never just a matter of not breaking rules or laws. That is, being ethical is never just a matter of being a good rule follower. It's exceedingly more than that.

Why? For starters, rules and laws by their very nature usually prescribe, at best, only *minimum* standards of ethical behavior. They are typically negative, telling us most often what we should not do rather than what we should do. They tell us that we cannot go over the speed limit, that we cannot take what is not rightfully ours, that we cannot knowingly falsify information, that we cannot discriminate against people on the basis of their ethnicity, gender, or religion, that we cannot cheat, and so forth.

So, rules and laws are usually very good and necessary when it comes to identifying what we should not do for our own (and society's) ethical good—in other words, they tell us how not to become bad. However, in and of themselves they do not usually tell us how to become people of good and virtuous character. They often prescribe, for example, how and when not to be disrespectful, but not how and when to be respectful; or they may prescribe how and when not to exploit those less fortunate than us, but not how and when to be charitable with the same people. And they seldom, if ever, tell us when and how to exhibit virtues like patience or love. Recalling the metaphorical language we use in Chapter 7: *Rules and laws tell us how to prevent weeds from growing in our gardens, but they don't usually tell us how to plant and cultivate roses.*

In addition, rules and laws (written ones in particular) can't possibly cover all the specific situations that arise in our day-to-day lives. Think for a moment about how true this is. How many rules and laws would we need to create in order to cover all possible human circumstances and eventualities? Imagine how overwhelmingly thick our rule books and law books would be!

There are many times when rules and laws give us little or no guidance as to an appropriate course of action. Codified law is often silent, for example, concerning the actions of people who use other people sexually (in contrast, the law is far from silent concerning the actions of people who use others financially). I have in mind here the not uncommon sort of situation in which an unwitting and sincere individual is "led on" emotionally and romantically by another, is eventually "dumped," and subsequently comes to the realization that the other person's motives were insincere and were directed only toward selfish sexual gratification. In short, an opportunistic and self-serving person has unfairly and harmfully exploited the heart, soul, and body of another. How many of us are going to disagree that using someone sexually in this way is not right?

This particular example brings to light at least three crucial points:

First, there are many behaviors, like sexual exploitation, that are clearly wrong even when they may not specifically be covered by written laws or rules. (There are countless other examples. Try thinking of as many other examples as you can; the process of doing so can be very enlightening.)

Second, in cases like this one, it will fall squarely and solely on our personal character to do the right thing, precisely because there are no written rules and laws explicitly "preventing" us from doing the wrong thing or explicitly "making" us do the right thing. Even if a rule or law happens to give us a general principle to follow, it will still be up to each of us and our individual personal character to carry out the right and specific course of action.

The third point is the insight captured by this chapter's title:

You can follow all the rules and still be unethical.

What this ultimately implies is that just because you and I might happen to follow all the rules and laws perfectly (assuming it is even possible to do so), dotting every *i* and crossing every *t* without fail, this by itself does not necessarily mean that you and I are ethical, are persons of good character, are good role models, and so forth. It would likely suggest something positive about our character, but not necessarily. There would still exist the distinct possibility that you and I have poor ethical character, despite the fact that we aren't habitual rule and law breakers. For example, we might turn out to be habitual prigs—self-righteous individuals who condescendingly look down on and belittle the lives of others.

Have you ever said to someone else, in defense of yourself, something such as, "How can you accuse me of being unethical when I didn't violate any rules?" Or have you ever done something questionable that you ultimately justified on the basis of this sort of reasoning?

Truth is, it's not that difficult to follow the rules and still be unethical. When we begin to think about the limited domain of codified rules and laws and about how many circumstances and actions are not specifically covered by codified rules and laws, we can begin to get a good grasp of the profound responsibility placed on our individual personal character.

To conclude this chapter, I share the following from a similar discussion in a book of mine focusing on personal character in sports:

> While I must have the character to play by the rules,
> I must also have the character
> to do the right thing when the rules don't help.
> If I want to have the character to be a good role model,
> then I must have the character
> to go above and beyond the rules.
> If I want to have the character
> to strive for ethical excellence,
> *then I must have the character*
> *to draw the line when there is no line drawn.*

CHAPTER THIRTEEN

Sow a thought, reap an act.
Sow an act, reap a habit.
Sow a habit, reap a character.
Sow a character, reap a destiny.

Anonymous

Consider the issues I have introduced and discussed in this book:

Examining your life

Improving what you are "in the dark"

Determining the course of your own ethical destiny

Taking responsibility for the final forming of your character

Having the courage to do what you know is right

Doing the right thing naturally and consistently

Making the pursuit of virtue your overarching aim

Becoming a better ethical role model

Being kinder and more respectful when speaking about the character of others

Having the character to draw the line where there is no line drawn

When it comes to taking seriously the personal ethics of your everyday life, there are few time-honored proverbs more exactingly true and reliable than this:

You reap what you sow.

What is particularly powerful about the oft-cited verse serving as our chapter title is the way in which it takes this proverb's elemental truth and breaks it down further into very concrete, step-by-step terms. With its five key words we have not only a concise, visual summary of this book's message but also, and more important, an easy-to-remember, basic formula for achieving ethical excellence:

Thought → Act → Habit → Character → Destiny

I strongly encourage you to write down the entire verse (or this formula) on a sheet of paper and put it in a conspicuous place in your home, office, or car, or wherever it can remind you daily of the meticulous sowing and reaping required to become a better person.

I especially would like you to consider toward the close of our discussion two intimately related capstone thoughts concerning this critical process of sowing and reaping. First, this thought:

Over the course of our lives, we ultimately reap far more from the little, seemingly mundane acts and choices we have sown daily than from the big, dramatic ones we have sown only occasionally.

Following from the first is this second thought:

Thus, the all-encompassing and most critical ethical challenge of our lives is working diligently, very diligently, day by day, moment by moment, act by act, to sow meaningful and enduring improvement in our personal character.

After reading these thoughts for the first time, you may think that they sound a bit bland. But perhaps you will find them inspiring when you consider the degree to which they represent two of the most realistic and indispensable insights I have shared with you—and are thus eminently well worth emphasizing here toward the close of our discussion.

The utter consequential nature, even the inspirational nature, of these thoughts was particularly impressed upon me in graduate school while reading for the first time a wonderful and relatively short ethics text by Ralph McInerny titled *Ethica Thomistica: The Moral Philosophy of Thomas Aquinas*. In the chapter "Character and Decision," amid a discussion of the central ethical importance of developing good habits (virtues), McInerny draws a provocative and most enlightening analogy between the process of changing one's character (for better or worse) and the process of falling into—and out of—love with someone.

He begins by recounting an episode described in the autobiography of a twentieth-century British philosopher (who is now deceased). In this autobiography, the philosopher describes how it "suddenly" occurred to him one day while he was out riding his bicycle that he no longer loved his wife. Here is McInerny's astute analysis of the story:

Now it is that "suddenly" that is of interest. It seems clear enough that such a realization could be sudden, but at the same time it seems right to say that what is being realized could not have come about suddenly, unless we wish to retain the Romantic myth that we fall in love like meteors hitting the earth and fall out of it as we sometimes fall out of bed. Even if there were truth to Romanticism, such thunderbolt alterations of who we are, what we are, the self that is ours, hardly seem paradigmatic of what it is like to come to a decision which is momentous for our lives.

It is an unsettling thought that decisions of an important kind, the kind we tend to concentrate on in doing [i.e., studying or discussing] ethics, are not simply a matter of assessing a situation in the light of principles and then deciding, but are in some mysterious way made before we make them. Does it not seem reasonable to assume that, when a man leaves his wife, or vice versa, the decision is the cumulative effect of a whole series of minor decisions, each of them, when taken singly, of little moment . . . which yet, in the aggregate, in unforeseen and also unintended combinations, constitute the person we are when the momentous decision is to be made? . . . [T]he moral life is a continuum, not episodic as if it were composed of discontinuous . . . moments. . . .

A man suddenly realizes that he no longer loves his wife, but the transition from faithful loving spouse to potential divorcé is scarcely sudden. In the halcyon early days of wedded life, the honeymoon, and beyond, a man strives and succeeds to see his life with reference to his beloved. He squelches impulses to act in a way inimical to their union; he overlooks and forgives actions destructive of unity and outlook. Two become one flesh, but more importantly, two autonomous human persons adopt a common outlook and aspiration. The goal they seek is to see the other, in the classic phrase, as *dimidium animae meae,* the other and complementary half of my soul. This is an achievement, of course, not something bestowed by the marriage ceremony or the sacrament. The achievement is seldom a matter of deeds of a dramatic sort. A whole congeries [collections] of actions which taken singly or viewed by an outsider are insignificant conspire to form an outlook, a shared outlook. The union of spouses is made up of such elements as reading the same books, attending the same Mass, quarreling and making up, conceiving children and raising them—a whole series of deeds which foster union or threaten it. One could go on. What then does it mean to say that suddenly a man realizes he no longer loves his wife? Is this like succumbing to a virus, getting a tan, a risk one runs when bicycling? One wonders who might be riding on the handlebars. Such things do not happen suddenly. A series of minor infidelities—perhaps scarcely approaching the status of velleities [mere intentions or desires]—imaginings, dreams of an elsewhere and otherwise brought on by disagreements of a more or less substantial sort, the encouragement of fantasy—these underlie the process. The process is gradual; the realization may indeed be sudden. But it is the realization of what one has voluntarily and responsibly brought about.

Please go back for a moment now and reread our two capstone thoughts.

After doing so, think long and hard about the ways in which the following key lines from the *Ethica Thomistica* passage forcefully amplify the fundamental and consequential nature of both capstone thoughts.

> . . . thunderbolt alterations of who we are, what we are, the self that is ours, hardly seem paradigmatic of what it is like to come to a decision which is momentous for our lives.

Consider: Even the dramatic and momentous decisions of my life are and will be determined primarily by my ingrained dispositions of character—those good and bad habits I have developed gradually, day by day, act by act.

> Does it not seem reasonable to assume that, when a man leaves his wife, or vice versa, the decision is the cumulative effect of a whole series of minor decisions, each of them, when taken singly, of little moment . . . which yet, in the aggregate, in unforeseen and also unintended combinations, constitute the person we are when the momentous decision is to be made? . . . [T]he moral life is a continuum, not episodic as if it were composed of discontinuous . . . moments.

Consider: More than anything else, who and what I presently am—my present personal character—as well as the actions presently flowing from my character are the result of (are a continuum of) the little and seemingly mundane acts and choices I have sown gradually and daily over the course of my life. Thus, in reality, my day-to-day acts and choices are anything but little and mundane—on the contrary, they determine my destiny.

> This is an achievement. . . . The achievement is seldom a matter of deeds of a dramatic sort.

Consider: My actions and decisions, however seemingly great or small, represent achievements in my life. They are achievements in the sense that I have, each passing day of my life, sown or worked toward—for better or worse, consciously or not—the constitution of my present character and the actions flowing from my present character.

> Such things do not happen suddenly. . . . The process is gradual. . . .

Consider: Again, as a very strong rule of thumb, even my most dramatic and momentous decisions are and will be primarily the result of a slow, gradual, day-by-day habit-building process.

> . . . it is the realization of what one has voluntarily and responsibly brought about.

Consider: This is precisely why the all-encompassing and most critical ethical challenge of my life is working diligently, very diligently, day by day, moment by moment, act by act, to sow meaningful and enduring improvement in my personal character—because when all is said and done, I and I alone voluntarily determine and am responsible for my ethical destiny.

One of the sobering and somewhat daunting realities is that changing and improving your present habits of character can be—likely will be—very hard work. And *that*, let there be no doubt, is precisely what the process is—*work*. There is nothing automatic about becoming a better person. There are no shortcuts involved. Remember: One isolated virtuous act, while praiseworthy, does not suddenly make a habitually unvirtuous person "virtuous." Only conscientious and persistent individual effort will yield meaningful and enduring results.

On the bright side, you unquestionably have the capacity to improve your personal character. Regardless of your age or how "set in your ways" you may be, and no matter what your external circumstances, you have the internal ability—and the responsibility—to choose and continually strive to be better.

The only question, now and forever, is: Do you have the *will* to do so?

CHAPTER FOURTEEN

I have found who is responsible for our ethical poverty, and it is I.

R. G.

As comedienne Joan Rivers would say: Can we talk?

Here, at the close of our conversation, can we, as friends, put all of our cards on the table? With no pretension or defensiveness, let's be utterly honest with each other and especially with ourselves about who is responsible for the ethical poverty endangering both our individual and collective destinies.

The odds are great that you and I—and virtually all Americans—strongly agree on two points regarding this issue, given the numerous studies and surveys in recent years. First, we strongly agree that our society is suffering from a poverty of "personal ethics," "personal character," "ethical and moral values," and "virtuous behavior." However it's described, we're all clearly concerned about the same disturbing disregard for what is right and good.

Second (and please keep thinking about being "utterly honest"), we also strongly agree about *who* is responsible for this ethical poverty: He is. She is. They are.

You are.

But not *me*.

And that, my friend, is one of our greatest, if not most lethal, ethical problems: I'm blaming you, and you're blaming me. We're blaming them, and they're blaming us. And the blame-throwing really is that bad.

Take, for instance, an eye-opening and in-depth article in the December 16, 1996, issue of *U.S. News & World Report*. Under the bold and unsettling title of "I'm OK, you're not: Why Americans think their lives are good but the nation is in peril," the article describes the results of a comprehensive survey showing that while the overwhelming majority of us believe our society is in serious trouble (especially from an ethical point of view), at the same time we do not believe this trouble is due to our own attitudes and behaviors.

In short, it's not my fault; it's someone else's fault. It's someone else's lack of personal character and ethics, not mine.

"The most striking feature of the I'm-OK-you're-not syndrome," the article explains, "may be its universality. Scholars are just as susceptible to it as are high-school dropouts. Rich, poor, black, white, young, old—virtually all groups of Americans simultaneously hold sanguine views of themselves and pessimistic views of others."

Let's admit it. Rather than being in the habit of looking in the moral mirror, as a culture—no, as *individuals*—we're in the habit of blaming someone else for our ethical poverty:

> Liberals blame conservatives; conservatives blame liberals.
>
> The majority blames the minority; the minority blames the majority.

The pro's blame the anti's; the anti's blame the pro's.

The haves blame the have nots; the have nots blame the haves.

Those who live in the city blame those who live in the suburbs; suburbanites blame city dwellers.

Men blame women; women blame men.

Children blame parents; parents blame children.

Neighbor blames neighbor.

Ethnicity blames ethnicity.

Employers blame employees; employees blame employers.

Students blame teachers; teachers blame students.

The young blame the old; the old blame the young.

And *everyone* blames politicians, lawyers, and the media.

You know what I'm talking about, right? And it's virtually unarguable, isn't it, concerning the disturbing degree to which we have become a culture of blamers and finger-pointers? Or concerning the almost comical, albeit serious, irony of imperfect moral beings habitually blaming imperfect moral beings? Of sinners habitually pointing the finger at sinners? Isn't there something quite ridiculous or embarrassing (choose your own adjective) about this rampant I'm-OK-you're-not state of affairs?

My point of course isn't the fanciful one that we don't have the right—or the responsibility—to challenge and constructively criticize the behaviors and policies of others simply because we're imperfect. We do have the right, and we certainly should challenge and constructively criticize when appropriate and necessary. Moreover, to even have and enjoy certain liberties and rights in the first place, we *must* hold each other accountable for our actions. But our biggest problem isn't a matter of holding others accountable; it's a matter of holding *ourselves* accountable.

For the title of this chapter, I have taken the old saying "We have met the enemy and it is us" and recast it:

I have found who is responsible
for our ethical poverty, and it is I.

Do you see why this is true?

If I don't keep my word; if I steal items (or time, which is money) from my employer; if I use people sexually; if I cheat on my taxes; if I use recreational (read: *illegal*) drugs; if I falsify insurance claims or expense reports; if I illicitly duplicate copyrighted products; if I'm constantly trying to "beat the system"; if I treat people badly simply because of their ethnicity, gender, religion, or socio-economic status; if I cheat on exams; if I'm always looking for legal loopholes; if I treat people merely as the means to my own selfish ends; if I'm justifying my unethical actions on the basis of "everyone else is doing it"; if I continue to spend money while neglecting to pay off my debts; if I'm unfaithful to loved ones; or if I just sit back and criticize society without lifting a finger to help, then in a real and concrete sense *I am responsible for our ethical poverty.*

My friend, in all seriousness, what kind of people are we if we don't have the character to own up to our own shortcomings and responsibilities? What has happened, what *is* happening, to the essential truth of President Truman's famous line "The buck stops here"?

Or of Thomas Carlyle's sentiment "The greatest of faults is to be conscious of none"?

Or of the version of the Golden Rule that says, "Judge others in a way that you would want to be judged"?

Or, in spiritual terms, of C. S. Lewis' poignant phrase " 'My heart'—I need no other's—'showeth me the wickedness of the ungodly' "?

Or, as I mentioned in the Introduction, of our founding fathers' passionate plea that democracy can only survive if its citizens—you and I—live with a higher degree of virtue? What happens when we all agree there's a serious problem but we're personally unwilling to take any responsibility for it?

Taking responsibility has an important, twofold meaning. It doesn't merely imply that I am a significant part of the *problem*. It also implies that I am a significant part of the *solution* to the problem.

For our own good and the common good—make no mistake, the two are deeply intertwined—at what point will we stop pointing the finger at each other and start habitually pointing it primarily and directly in the direction of our own personal mirrors? When will we do this? Today? Tomorrow? Never? (God help us!)

Now?

Let there be no doubt: As long as we continue to blame others instead of assuming responsibility ourselves, there will be no meaningful and enduring change for the better—neither in our personal lives nor in our society generally.

That's why it's no exaggeration to say that what we've been discussing throughout this book is the *essential* value of personal ethics in everyday life. Issues of personal ethics—character—cut to the core of our greatest personal and social responsibilities and endeavors.

Doing the right thing simply because it is the right thing certainly represents the highest degree of virtue and thus should be our ultimate ethical goal (or, as many throughout the ages have said, that virtue should be its own reward). However, we should not overlook or underestimate or even downplay the fact that it is in your and my best personal interests, just as it is in our best collective interest, to strive to be individuals of excellent ethical character.

We're simply deceiving ourselves and others if we try to argue that being ethical has nothing to do with being practical. It absolutely does. It has to. If not, then why in the world do we "sow"? We sow to *reap*.

Recalling the theme of Chapter 7 (on the importance of focusing primarily on virtue), I'm concerned that we tend to spend too much time trying to convince ourselves that "crime doesn't pay" and far too little time convincing ourselves that virtue does in fact "pay." Please don't misunderstand: I'm not making the facile and *unvirtuous* point that we should strive to improve our personal character in order to become rich and famous. That's emphatically not my point. What I'm trying to drive home is that we sow to reap, and the "harvest"—both individually and as a society—*is much more deeply and enduringly valuable, useful, and fulfilling when we act ethically as a matter of habit in our daily lives.*

The truth, the real truth, is that life rewards those who are ethical. Life gives rewards in different ways and in varying degrees, but it does reward:

Our academic or athletic or artistic skills improve dramatically if we are *diligent* and *confident.*

Business relationships are stronger and more productive if we are people of *integrity* and *responsibility.*

Our ability to work with and learn from other people is significantly enhanced if we continually exhibit *patience* and *respect.*

Marriage and romance are immeasurably richer if we have the character to be *humble*, *understanding*, and *true* to our promises and commitments.

Our strong and ongoing disagreements with others are much more manageable and constructive and much less stressful and destructive when we consistently have the *courage* to disagree with *civility.*

Our health, both physical and emotional, is improved and sustained in direct proportion to our ability to show, as a matter of daily habit, *self-discipline* and *balance.*

Our friendships grow in depth and meaningfulness
if we are persons who can accurately be described
as *dependable* and *empathetic.*

Our capacity to become more effective leaders
is greatly enhanced if we can develop the habit
of *listening* and the habit of showing *poise* in
the face of criticism or adversity.

Our own sense of purpose and place will
dramatically intensify as we learn to be
more *compassionate* and *generous* to those
around us who are hurting and lonely.

Our spiritual commitments and goals become
more palpable and life-enriching as we strive
to cultivate the virtues of *faith* and *hope.*

All in all, our well-being and happiness will be—can only be—meaningfully and enduringly enhanced if we take seriously the personal ethics of our everyday lives. "Every little action of the common day makes or unmakes character." This is a simple though penetrating sentiment of the nineteenth-century writer Oscar Wilde.

From me to you, friend to friend: May you have the will to transform every little action of your common day into the making of your personal character.

An Ethics Checklist

1. Is it in compliance with the law or any written rules?
2. Is it fair to everyone involved?
3. Would my ethical role model do it?

In this book, I have focused primarily on that vast majority of times in our daily lives when we have a pretty clear idea of the ethical line separating the right thing to do from the wrong thing to do. Thus, our discussion has been one not of knowing the right thing to do but of *having the character to do the right thing.*

Now, it is an all-too-obvious fact of life that we will be faced occasionally with difficult ethical situations in which we truly won't know where the ethical line is drawn or we truly won't know what is most ethically appropriate to do. Fortunately, these difficult situations—"ethical dilemmas," as we refer to them—are the exception rather than the rule in our lives (for the overwhelming majority of us anyway).

Even if they don't happen that often, they *do* happen; and when they do, they're far from pleasant. Genuine ethical dilemmas can present us with some of the most gut-wrenching and mind-numbing decisions that we will ever have to make.

I'm offering this ethics checklist as an easy-to-remember tool that can effectively help you work toward a resolution of many of the ethical dilemmas you might face. Keep in mind, however, that there are no absolutely fail-safe methods for resolving ethical dilemmas. They're not like algebra problems for which we can count on a given formula to unfailingly give us the right answer.

Nonetheless, even if the checklist doesn't immediately give you the right answer, much of the time it can point you in the right direction. And, it seems to me, that's half the battle when it comes to confronting ethical dilemmas.

I would suggest two rules of thumb concerning how to use this checklist. First, ask the three questions in the order they are given. This may not be necessary, but it seems fairly logical, especially by beginning with civil law or concrete written rules. In most cases, if the contemplated action is explicitly against the law or established rules, there's probably little reason to proceed further through the checklist!

Second—and this is a very strong rule of thumb—if you answer no to any one of the three questions, then stop and reflect for several minutes (certainly, if you answer no to *more* than one question, you would be well advised to stop and think at this point). You very likely already have reason enough for *not* doing the act in question. Once you reach this conclusion, then it becomes a matter of you having the strength and courage of personal character to put your conscientious judgment into action.

So, if you find yourself in a situation in which you need to determine what is ethically appropriate, ask yourself the questions in this checklist:

1. Is it in compliance with the law or any written rules?
    - Civil law?
    - Company or institutional policies?
    - Rules of the game?
    - Religious law?
    - Family rules?
    - Other rules?

2. Is it fair to everyone involved?
    - To my family?
    - To my friends?
    - To my colleagues or coworkers?
    - To my employer?
    - To my community?
    - To those less fortunate than me?
    - To others?

3. Would my ethical role model do it?
    - Who *is* my ethical role model?
    - How would that person feel about me if I did it?
    - How would I feel about that person if he/she did it?
    - Do I have time to get that person's advice first?
    - Do I have the courage to do what that person would do?

Notes

CHAPTER ONE

p 6 *For example, because of their interest in ethics and moral education . . .* To name two of the most influential developmental psychologists in the field of moral education: William Damon, author of *Greater Expectations: Overcoming the Culture of Indulgence in Our Homes and Schools* (New York: Free Press, 1995), and Thomas Lickona, author of *Educating for Character: How Our Schools Can Teach Respect and Responsibility* (New York: Simon & Schuster, 1991).

p 7 *Nonetheless, problems in our collective understanding and confusions in our language do exist . . .* My discussion here is indebted to Daniel Taylor's insightful discussion of character and personality in his eloquent book *The Healing Power of Stories: Creating Yourself Through the Stories of Your Life* (New York: Doubleday, 1996), specifically Chapter 3, "Characters Shaping Character: Beyond Personality," 41–56.

p 9 *For all the understandable emphasis and attention that our culture continues to give self-esteem . . .* For the best critical discussion of self-esteem that I have read to date, see Damon, *Greater Expectations*, Chapter 4.

p 9 *In a widely acclaimed investigation of the rescuers of Jews during the Holocaust . . .* Sam and Pearl Oliner, *The Altruistic Personality* (New York: The Free Press, 1988).

p 10 *"Certain forms of high self-esteem . . ."* Roy Baumeister, Laura Smart, and Joseph Boden, "Relation of Threatened Egotism to Violence and Aggression: The Dark Side of High Self-Esteem," *Psychological Review* 103, no. 1 (January 1996), 5–33.

CHAPTER TWO

p 17 *"I will not cease from philosophy . . ."* Plato, *Apology*, 29d, 30a.

p 21 *"Know your major defect. . . ."* Baltasar Gracian, *The Art of Worldly Wisdom*, trans. Christopher Maurer (New York: Doubleday, 1992), 127.

p 21 *"Know yourself: your character . . ."* Ibid., 50–51.

CHAPTER THREE

p 29 *"There is, for better or worse . . ."* Ralph McInerny, *Ethica Thomistica: The Moral Philosophy of Thomas Aquinas* (Washington, D.C.: The Catholic University of America, 1982), 92.

CHAPTER FOUR

p 39 *"I have one outstanding trait . . ."* Anne Frank, *The Diary of a Young Girl* (New York: Doubleday & Co., 1952), 274–275.

CHAPTER FIVE

p 49 *Over 150 years later . . .* Robert Coles, "The Disparity Between Intellect and Character," *The Chronicle of Higher Education* (September 22, 1995), A68. Unless noted otherwise, all direct quotations related to Professor Coles' anecdote in this chapter are excerpted from this one-page essay.

p 49 *The student, named Marian . . .* Coles does not use Marian's name in his *Chronicle* essay. While relating the very same story, however, he does name her in his most recent (and excellent) book: *The Moral Intelligence of Children* (New York: Random House, 1997), 178–184.

p 51 *"She was pointedly reminding me . . ."* Coles, *The Moral Intelligence of Children*, 181–182.

p 55 *"A great deal of a child's moral life . . ."* William Kilpatrick, *Why Johnny Can't Tell Right from Wrong: Moral Illiteracy and the Case for Character Education* (New York: Simon & Schuster, 1992), 85.

p 56 *Consider these telling results . . .* The study was conducted in 1996 by the Josephson Institute of Ethics, based in Marina del Rey, California.

CHAPTER SEVEN

p 75 *"Trying to become virtuous . . ."* Donald DeMarco, *The Heart of Virtue: Lessons from Life and Literature Illustrating the Beauty and Value of Moral Character* (San Francisco: Ignatius Press, 1996), 13–14.

CHAPTER NINE

p 97 *"How is this rare quality . . ."* Anne Colby and William Damon, *Some Do Care: Contemporary Lives of Moral Commitment* (New York: The Free Press, 1992), 7–8.

p 101 *Thanks in large measure . . .* See the Introduction for a discussion on the Aristotelian use of "friend" and "friendship."

CHAPTER TEN

p 110 *"The greatness of Schweitzer . . ."* Norman Cousins, *Albert Schweitzer's Mission* (New York: W. W. Norton & Co., 1984), 303–304.

p 110 *"Albert Schweitzer is a spiritual immortal. . . ."* Ibid., 139, 140.

p 112 *"Every life is a profession of faith . . ."* Henri Frederic Amiel, as quoted in *Who Said That?*, ed. George Sweeting (Chicago: Moody Press, 1995), 179.

CHAPTER ELEVEN

p 122 *"Invariably, a minority raise their hands . . ."* Joseph Telushkin, *Words That Hurt, Words That Heal: How to Choose Words Wisely and Well* (New York: William Morrow and Company, Inc., 1996), xvii–xviii.

p 124 *"Don't be a blacklist of others' faults. . . ."* Baltasar Gracian, *The Art of Worldly Wisdom*, trans. Christopher Maurer (New York: Doubleday, 1992), 70.

p 125 *"In a small Eastern European town . . ."* Telushkin, *Words That Hurt, Words That Heal,* 3.

p 127 *"[B]efore you assert this as a definite fact . . ."* Ibid., xviii.

CHAPTER TWELVE

p 138 *"While I must have the character . . ."* Russell Gough, *Character Is Everything: Promoting Ethical Excellence in Sports* (Fort Worth: Harcourt Brace College Publishers, 1997), 88.

CHAPTER THIRTEEN

p 139 *"Sow a thought . . ."* A few sources attribute this popular verse to the nineteenth-century English writer Charles Reade. After a fairly thorough search at my university's library, I discovered that we really do not know for sure with whom this verse originated, thus, my designation of "Anonymous."

p 144 *"Now it is that 'suddenly' that is of interest . . ."* Ralph McInerny, *Ethica Thomistica: The Moral Philosophy of Thomas Aquinas* (Washington, D.C.: The Catholic University of America, 1982), 93–96.